Tournaments, Risk and Careers

Inauguraldissertation

zur

Erlangung des Doktorgrades

der Wirtschafts- und Sozialwissenschaftlichen Fakultät

der Universität zu Köln

2008

vorgelegt von

Diplom-Kauffrau Petra Nieken

aus

Linnich

Referent: Professor Dr. Dirk Sliwka

Koreferent: Professor Dr. Thomas Hartmann-Wendels

Tag der Promotion: 19.12.2008

Berichte aus der Betriebswirtschaft

Petra Nieken

Tournaments, Risk and Careers

D 38 (Diss. Universität zu Köln)

Shaker Verlag
Aachen 2009

Bibliographic information published by the Deutsche Nationalbibliothek
The Deutsche Nationalbibliothek lists this publication in the Deutsche Nationalbibliografie; detailed bibliographic data are available in the Internet at http://dnb.d-nb.de.

Zugl.: Köln, Univ., Diss., 2008

ISBN 978-3-8322-7962-2
ISSN 0945-0696

Shaker Verlag GmbH • P.O. BOX 101818 • D-52018 Aachen
Phone: 0049/2407/9596-0 • Telefax: 0049/2407/9596-9
Internet: www.shaker.de • e-mail: info@shaker.de

Für meine Eltern und für Michael

Danksagung

Viele Menschen haben zur Entstehung dieser Arbeit beigetragen. Zunächst danke ich der Deutschen Forschungsgemeinschaft für die finanzielle Unterstützung im Rahmen des Graduiertenkollegs "Theoretische und empirische Grundlagen des Risikomanagements" sowie der Projekte IR 43/1-1 und KR 2077/2-3.

Mein besonderer Dank geht an meinen Doktorvater Dirk Sliwka für seine außergewöhnliche und sehr engagierte Betreuung. Er hat mich von Anfang an voll unterstützt und mir so den Start in die Forschung wesentlich erleichtert. Außerdem danke ich Thomas Hartmann-Wendels für seine Bereitschaft meine Doktorarbeit als Zweitgutachter zu bewerten.

Ich danke auch meinen Koautoren Matthias Kräkel und Judith Przemeck für die vielen spannenden Diskussionen und unzähligen Telefonate. Bernd Irlenbusch, Oliver Gürtler und Patrick Schmitz danke ich für die interessanten Gespräche und hilfreichen Tipps. Besonderer Dank geht an meine Kolleginnen und Kollegen Johannes Berger, Kathrin Breuer, René Fahr, Petra Gerlach, Christine Harbring, Patrick Kampkötter, Kathrin Manthei, Tom McKenzie, Alwine Mohnen und Nannan Zhou für die gute Zusammenarbeit und die tolle Arbeitsatmosphäre. Weiterhin danke ich unserer Sekretärin Beate Ommer sowie den wissenschaftlichen und studentischen Hilfskräften Tim Bartel, Stefan Degen, Behnud Djawadi, Andrea Hammermann, Elmar Janssen, Klemens Keldenich, Susi Kusche, Christiane Schäfer, Kai Seifert und Julia Sohn für ihre Unterstützung und Hilfsbereitschaft. Unseren Programmierern Anastasia Danilov, Naum Kocherovskiy und Andreas Staffeld danke ich für ihr Engagement bei Experimenten und ihre Geduld, wenn das Design doch noch mal geändert werden musste.

Ich danke meinen Freunden und meiner Familie, die mich bei dieser Arbeit immer unterstützt haben. Mein besonderer Dank gilt meinen Eltern, die immer hinter mir stehen und mich jederzeit unterstützen. Ohne diese Unterstützung hätte ich diese Arbeit nie begonnen.

Mein letzter und wichtigster Dank geht an meinen Freund Michael Stegh, ohne den diese Arbeit in jeder Hinsicht nicht zu dem geworden wäre, was sie heute ist. Ich danke ihm für die selbstlose Unterstützung und die unzähligen Tipps und Hilfestellungen, die er mir während der letzten Jahre gegeben hat. Durch seine Ruhe und Ausgeglichenheit habe ich viel Kraft gewonnen.

Contents

1 Introduction   **1**

2 Risk-Taking in Tournaments with Correlated Outcomes   **11**

     2.1   Introduction 11

     2.2   Theoretical Analysis 13

         2.2.1   The Model 13

         2.2.2   Equilibrium Analysis 14

     2.3   Experimental Design and Procedure 20

     2.4   Hypotheses 22

     2.5   Results 24

     2.6   Conclusion 30

     2.7   Appendix to Chapter 2 31

3 Risk-Taking and Effort in Tournaments with Homogeneous Agents   **45**

     3.1   Introduction 45

     3.2   Theoretical Analysis 47

         3.2.1   The Model 47

         3.2.2   Equilibrium Analysis 48

     3.3   Experimental Design and Procedure 50

     3.4   Hypotheses 53

     3.5   Results 54

     3.6   Discussion 64

     3.7   Conclusion 67

     3.8   Appendix to Chapter 3 69

4   Risk-Taking and Effort in Tournaments with Heterogeneous Agents   **83**

    4.1   Introduction 83

    4.2   The Game 86

    4.3   Discouragement Effect, Cost Effect and Likelihood Effect . . . 90

    4.4   Experimental Design and Procedure 93

    4.5   Hypotheses 95

    4.6   Experimental Results 97

          4.6.1   The Risk Stage 97

          4.6.2   The Effort Stage 99

    4.7   Discussion 103

    4.8   Conclusion 105

    4.9   Appendix to Chapter 4 107

5   Management Changes, Career Concerns and Earnings Management   **129**

    5.1   Introduction 129

    5.2   The Model 131

    5.3   Equilibrium Analysis 133

    5.4   Empirical Evidence and Testable Implications 136

    5.5   Conclusion 138

    5.6   Appendix to Chapter 5 139

Bibliography   **142**

List of Tables

2.1   Probit regressions for leading players in treatment 1   25

2.2   Probit regressions for treatment 2   27

2.3   Probit regression for leading players in treatment 3   29

2.4   Distribution of strategy choices for all treatments   33

2.5   Probit regressions for leading players in treatment 1, marginal effects reported   33

2.6   Probit regressions with random effects for leading players in treatment 1   34

2.7   Probit regressions for leading players in treatment 1 controlling for risk attitude   34

2.8   Probit regressions for treatment 2, marginal effects reported .   35

2.9   Probit regressions with random effects for treatment 2   35

2.10   Probit regressions for treatment 2 controlling for risk attitude   36

2.11   Probit regression for leading players in treatment 3, marginal effects reported   37

2.12   Probit regression with random effects for leading players in treatment 3   37

2.13   Probit regression for leading players in treatment 3 controlling for risk attitude   38

3.1   Regressions for effort dependent on state   55

3.2   One sample mean comparison test   56

3.3   Regressions for effort dependent on choice of risk of the players   60

3.4   Mean and standard deviation difference between player's belief and partner's effort   61

3.5   Mean of difference between effort and theoretical effort by state and subperiod   63

3.6   Regressions for choice of effort dependent on state   71

3.7   Fraction of the risk attitude of the players   72

3.8   Wilcoxon matched-pairs signed rank test for condition 2a and 2b   73

3.9   Regressions for choice of effort dependent on choice of risk of the players   73

3.10   Regressions for belief dependent on state   74

3.11   Regressions for choice of risk dependent on the risk attitude of the players   75

3.12   Cost table   81

4.1   Results on risk-taking   98

4.2   Results on effort choices   101

4.3   Results on effort comparisons   102

4.4   Comparison of the favorite's risk choices over treatments . . .   109

4.5   Probit regression Hypothesis 4: Comparison of the favorite's risk-taking in the cost and discouragement treatment   110

4.6   Probit regression Hypothesis 5: Comparison of the favorite's risk-taking in the discouragement and the likelihood treatment   111

4.7   Probit regression Hypothesis 6: Comparison of the favorite's risk-taking in the cost and likelihood treatment   112

4.8   Effort choices in the discouragement treatment high risk . . .   113

4.9   Effort choices in the discouragement treatment low risk   114

4.10   Effort choices in the discouragement treatment pooled data . .   115

4.11   Effort choices in the cost treatment high risk   116

4.12   Effort choices in the cost treatment low risk   117

4.13   Effort choices in the cost treatment pooled data   118

4.14   Effort choices in the likelihood treatment high risk   119

4.15   Effort choices in the likelihood treatment low risk   120

4.16   Effort choices in the likelihood treatment pooled data   121

4.17   Probit regression Hypothesis 7: Discouragement treatment . .   122

iv

4.18 Probit regression Hypothesis 7: Cost treatment 123

4.19 Probit regression Hypothesis 7: Likelihood treatment 124

List of Figures

2.1 Nash Equilibria of the game 19

2.2 Equilibrium mixed strategies if rho=1 23

2.3 Choice of risk for each treatment 24

2.4 Choice of the risky strategy for different leads in treatment 1 26

2.5 Choice of risk in treatment 2 36

2.6 Normal Distribution 42

2.7 Correlation coefficient of zero 43

2.8 Correlation coefficient of one 43

2.9 Correlation coefficient of 0.5 44

3.1 Mean of effort and standard deviation sorted by state 54

3.2 Fraction of the choice of state for two subperiods 58

3.3 Mean of effort and standard deviation sorted by state with
state 2 divided in state 2a and state 2b 59

3.4 Mean of difference between belief of the player and effort of
partner by state 62

3.5 Histogram of the risk attitude of the players 71

3.6 Mean of effort sorted by state and subperiods 72

3.7 Reaction function 74

3.8 State A (low variance) 79

3.9 State B (high variance) 80

3.10 Overview of both distributions 80

3.11 Costfunction 82

4.1 Discouragement effect 91

4.2 Likelihood effect 92

4.3   Comparison of the favorite's risk choices over treatments . . . 109

4.4   Effort choices in the discouragement treatment high risk . . . 113

4.5   Effort choices in the discouragement treatment low risk 114

4.6   Effort choices in the discouragement treatment pooled data . . 115

4.7   Effort choices in the cost treatment high risk 116

4.8   Effort choices in the cost treatment low risk 117

4.9   Effort choices in the cost treatment pooled data 118

4.10 Effort choices in the likelihood treatment high risk 119

4.11 Effort choices in the likelihood treatment low risk 120

4.12 Effort choices in the likelihood treatment pooled data 121

Chapter 1

Introduction

This thesis is about risk and uncertainty in careers. The following four chapters investigate different questions dealing with risk and uncertainty concerning tournaments, winner-take-all contests and earnings management during managerial turnover. The issues of risk and uncertainty in economics are manifold. In this thesis we concentrate on two main topics. First we investigate the risk-taking of agents in winner-take-all contests or tournaments such as job promotions or political elections. Second we analyze the consequences of uncertainty about talent for the reported earnings surrounding management changes in a career concerns model. Hence, the thesis can be divided into two parts. The first part encompasses the following three chapters and analyzes the active decisions about risk while the second part (the last chapter) of this thesis deals with the consequences of (exogenous) uncertainty for careers. We will first discuss some general background literature for part one before giving a more detailed description of each chapter belonging to this part of the thesis. Afterwards we will discuss the general background literature related to the second part and then elaborate on the details of the corresponding chapter.

The first part deals with risk-taking in tournaments and winner-take-all contests. We provide theoretical and experimental evidence on three research questions. First we investigate risk-taking in tournaments if the risky strategies are correlated. Second we study the behavior of homogeneous

1

agents in a two-stage tournament consisting of a risk and an effort stage. We conclude this part by analyzing such a two-stage tournament with unilateral risk-taking and heterogeneous agents.

In tournaments, agents compete against each other for a given set of prizes. The winner gets the high winner prize and the loser the lower loser prize. Many situations in the real world have the structure of tournaments. Typical examples are sports contests (Szymanski (2003)) or singing contests (Amegashie (2007)) where only one participant can win the final round. Or consider promotion tournaments where the agents compete for being promoted to the next career level (Baker et al. (1994) or DeVaro (2006)). Further examples are employees competing for bonuses (Murphy et al. (2004)) or fund managers competing for their clients' capital (Taylor (2003)). Firms are often involved in Research and Development races (Zhou (2006)) or in litigation contests for brand names or patent rights (Waerneryd (2000)).[1]

Most of the tournament models are based upon the seminal work of Lazear and Rosen (1981) who use a simple model with two risk-neutral agents to show that tournaments can induce efficient effort levels. In their model the agents' output is distorted by a random term which represents individual risk such as measurement error or luck. Hence, the output of the agents depends not only on their effort but on their individual risk component as well. However, the agents can only choose their effort and not the distribution of their individual risk. Lazear and Rosen (1981) show that in equilibrium, exerted effort depends on the difference between the winner and the loser prize. Furthermore, effort decreases if the random error component (individual risk) has an increased influence on the output. The work of Lazear and Rosen (1981) has been extended by many other researchers in several ways. See for example Green and Stokey (1983) or Nalebuff and Stiglitz (1983) who reveal the predominance of tournaments in an environment with common shocks. O'Keeffe et al. (1984) investigate the appropriate design of the prize structure of a tournament which is used for sorting purposes. Clark and Riis (1998) and Moldovanu and Sela (2001) analyze tournaments with more than two types of prizes.

---

[1] For a survey on tournaments and contests see e.g. Konrad (2007).

There exists a huge number of empirical studies comparing the predictions of tournament theory to empirical data. For example Knoeber and Thurman (1994) investigate the performance of broiler producers who are compensated according to their relative performance. Their results show that changes in prize levels which leave the prize spreads unchanged do not affect the performance of the broiler producers. There are also several studies dealing with executive compensation in organizations, see for example O'Reilly et al. (1988) or Main et al. (1993) who show that prize differences increase with the number of participants in tournaments. The analysis of Eriksson (1999) reveals that, in line with tournament theory, pay differences increase with the hierarchy level of an organization. Furthermore, Lee et al. (2008) show that higher wage dispersion, or in the terms of a tournament a higher prize spread, leads to higher performance of the organization.

While it is comparatively difficult to observe effort in organizations, this is easier in sports contests where the tournament structure is naturally given by the design of the game and performance is relatively easy to measure by final scores. These studies generally confirm the prediction of tournament theory, especially that higher performance can be induced by an increase in the prize spread. Ehrenberg and Bognanno (1990) and Orszag (1994) analyze data from the men's United States Professional Golf Association tour. While Ehrenberg and Bognanno (1990) use data from 1984 and find that scores are lower (performance is better) if the prize level is high, Orszag (1994), using data from 1992, contradicts these results. This is attributed to different handling of variables concerning weather. Fernie and Metcalf (1999) check the impact of different jockeys' contracts on performance while Sunde (2003) investigates the influence of the heterogeneity of male tennis professionals in ATP tournaments on their effort.

Yet in real-world tournaments, the agents often not only choose their effort but have the opportunity to decide about the risk of their behavior as well. For instance, a fund manager can decide whether to invest in stocks with a high or a low volatility. Athletes have the option to try a new (and often more risky) training method or to stick to the old standard method. Before firms decide about their advertising budget they have to determine

3

whether they will implement a new product line or keep the old one. And in politics the "gambling for resurrection" phenomenon is often observed as political leaders who fear defeat in an election sometimes may choose a risky political agenda to reverse their fate. Often agents first choose between a high-risk strategy and a low-risk one and then decide on their input to win the tournament or contest.

Previous work on risk-taking in tournaments can be divided into two strands. The first strand skips the effort stage and deals solely with the choice of risk in tournaments. This setting fits best for mutual fund managers or other agents who can only influence their outcome in a tournament by deciding about risk. For example Gaba and Kalra (1999) investigate the risk-taking behavior of sales representatives who are paid according to quota-based or contest-based compensation schemes. While Hvide and Kristiansen (2003) study the selection efficiency of tournaments where risk is the choice variable, Taylor (2003) analyzes the behavior of mutual fund managers either competing with an index or with another mutual fund manager. There are also numerous examples of papers examining the risk choice of mutual fund managers empirically, see for example Brown et al. (1996) or Chevalier and Ellison (1997). Additionally there are also some papers in the sport-contest world which deal with risk-taking empirically. For instance, Becker and Huselid (1992) investigate individual behavior in stock-car racing. They show that drivers take more risk if the tournament prizes and the spread of these prizes are high. The research from Bothner et al. (2007) on car racing reveals that drivers are more likely to crash their cars if their position is endangered by a nearby and lower ranked participant.

While the first strand of the literature skips the effort stage, the second strand probes two-stage tournaments with risk-taking at the first stage and the choice of effort at the second stage. We will discuss this literature only briefly here and elaborate on the papers in Chapter 3 and 4 of this thesis. Hvide (2002) analyzes a two-stage tournament with homogeneous agents whereas Kräkel and Sliwka (2004) combine the choice of risk with asymmetry in tournaments. In both settings the equilibria of the effort stage are symmetric. In contrast Kräkel (forthcoming) investigates an uneven tourna-

4

ment and shows that other types of equilibria at the effort stage are possible in addition to the symmetric equilibria. One of the central findings of these papers is that the decision about risk has an influence on the effort chosen by the agents. To the best of our knowledge there exist no empirical papers investigating such two-stage tournaments. The main reason for this gap in the literature is perhaps that effort decisions are not easy to observe and measure in the field. There are also no experimental studies that explicitly deal with risk-taking in tournaments. Of course there are many experimental studies investigating behavior in tournaments and comparing for example tournaments with piece rate systems (Bull et al. (1987) and Wu and Roe (2005)) or tournament size with prize structure (Harbring and Irlenbusch (2003)). Bull et al. (1987) are among the first to analyze tournament situations in the laboratory. In their studies several treatments with different variances in the random shock have been investigated. Yet they vary the spread of the prize as well to induce the same equilibrium effort in each treatment. Therefore, they are unable to test if the change in the variance of the random shock leads ceteris paribus to an adjusted effort. This gap in the existing literature is one of the reasons why this thesis deals with risk-taking in tournaments.

We now discuss the content of the chapters belonging to part one in more detail. In Chapter 2 we focus on risk-taking in tournaments if the risky strategies are correlated. We first develop a theoretical model and then test its predictions in a controlled laboratory experiment. In our model the agents with different abilities can choose between a risky and a safe strategy. In the classical tournament models (see for example Lazear and Rosen (1981)) the random or risk components of the agents are not correlated. These models disregard the possibility that the risk component may symbolize, for example, the risk of an election campaign or an investment choice and therefore risk is a choice variable. If the available options are all very similar to each other it may occur that they choose the same or closely related options. Therefore, in our model we allow the risky strategies to be correlated between zero and one. We develop a simple tournament in which two contestants can choose between a safe or a risky option and analyze the possible equilibria. The key intuition often expressed that a favorite (the agent with a lead) should aim for

5

the safe option whereas the underdog in the competition has an incentive to choose the risky strategy does not always hold. Our main theoretical findings show that the chosen option strongly depends on the correlation of the risky options and on the difference between the abilities of the favorite and the underdog. The theoretical predictions are tested in a controlled laboratory experiment. We run three different treatments each dealing with a different correlation of the risky strategies. In the first treatment the risky strategies are uncorrelated, in the second treatment they are perfectly correlated and in the third treatment the correlation coefficient is $\frac{1}{2}$. Each treatment lasts 23 rounds and we vary the ability of the contestants in each round. Our results support the theoretical prediction that the chosen strategy strongly depends on the correlation of the outcomes of the risky strategy.

In the second chapter we have skipped the effort choice and have concentrated solely on the choice of risk if the outcomes of the risky strategy are correlated. As already mentioned in many real world situations agents not only decide about risk but also about the effort they exert in a tournament or contest. Hence, in Chapter 3 we investigate such a two-stage tournament with risk choice in the first stage and the choice of effort in the second stage in a controlled laboratory experiment. Based on the theoretical work of Hvide (2002) and Kräkel and Sliwka (2004) we analyze a simple two-stage tournament and focus on homogeneous agents. Because the equilibrium at the second stage where the agents decide about effort is symmetric and the agents are homogeneous, the winning probability is not affected by the risk choice in the first stage. Hence, the choice of risk only influences the amount of effort chosen and therefore also the costs of effort (cost effect). As the amount of effort declines ceteris paribus if the risk is higher, the agents prefer to choose high risk in order to reduce their costs of effort. Since this result is not intuitive at first glance we test the theoretical predictions in a controlled laboratory experiment in this chapter. In this experiment both agents first choose the amount of risk and then, after observing the risk choice of their opponent, decide about their effort. Our results reveal that indeed the players reduce their effort if the risk is high. However, they do not prefer the high-risk option at the first stage, which contradicts theory. Interestingly the

6

players decide about their effort solely based on their own choice of risk and do not take into account the overall risk.

While the third chapter deals with homogeneous agents who are both risk takers at the first stage, Chapter 4 investigates a two-stage tournament with heterogeneous agents where only a single first mover chooses risk in the first stage. Such a situation may for example occur if there are two politicians competing in an election campaign. Often there is an incumbent politician who stands for a certain well-known agenda and a challenger who first has to choose the risk of his agenda before both politicians simultaneously invest their resources during the election campaign. Our model, which is based on Kräkel (forthcoming), shows that the intuition for the favorite to prefer low risk and the underdog high risk is not necessarily true. The experimental analysis focuses on the risk-taking of the favorite and the effort choices of both contestants as the risk-taking of the favorite leads to much more interesting predictions than the risk-taking of the underdog. Regarding the risk choice of the favorite we can differentiate between three effects. First, as in Chapter 3, risk-taking at the first stage may influence effort at the second stage (cost effect). Second, with asymmetric agents the choice of risk may also influence the likelihood of winning. If equilibrium effort does not depend on risk-taking the favorite will prefer low risk to maintain his leading position (likelihood effect). Third, if effort depends on risk-taking the favorite may select high risk to win (discouragement effect). In the experiment we run one treatment for each effect and our results indicate that contrary to the discouragement effect, both the effort effect and the likelihood effect are relevant for the players when deciding about risk. Furthermore, as in Chapter 3, the effort choices are very often in line with the theory.

The second part of this thesis investigates the consequences of uncertainty about the talent of the managers for the earnings management during management turnover. In contrast to the first part of this thesis where the agents decide about the risk they are willing to take, in this part the uncertainty is exogenously given. We study earnings management and its connection to pre-announced managerial turnover in a career concerns model. These career concerns models build on the work of Fama (1980) and Holmström

7

(1982) who show that career concerns are an important incentive device. Dewatripont et al. (1999a) and Dewatripont et al. (1999b) extend Holström's framework by including for instance multiple tasks or a more general production function. As in the setting of Holmström (1982) and Holmström (1999) the ability of the managers is unknown for all participants, hence there is uncertainty about the talent of the manager. Because the market participants derive their assessment of the ability from the reported earnings, the managers may have an incentive to bias accounting data in order to appear highly talented. Normally, external reporting or accounting has the purpose of reducing the information asymmetry between organizations and market participants. However, accounting statements are not always reliable due to manipulation by the managers in charge.

There are several reasons why managers might influence reported earnings that are discussed in literature (see e.g. Dechow and Skinner (2000), Beneish (2001) or Bergstresser and Philippon (2006)). The managers could for example try to smooth earnings to give the market the impression of stable earnings or secure their jobs (Fudenberg and Tirole (1995) or DeFond and Park (1997)). On the other hand managers may bias reported earnings to maximize their own bonus payments. This so-called bonus-plan hypothesis was first investigated by Healy (1985). Since then there have been many other studies that examine the effect of compensation contracts on earnings management (see for example Guidry et al. (1999) or Baker et al. (2003)) indicating that managers indeed use accounting methods to increase earnings-based bonus rewards (Healy and Wahlen (1999)). As Shuto (2007) has shown, the association between discretionary accruals and executive compensation depends on the circumstances of the organization. Depending on the design of the contract, managers try to maximize their utility either by increasing or by decreasing the current reported earnings. If, for instance, earnings have to meet a certain performance threshold, reported earnings are decreased if managers are not able to meet this threshold. Hence, nonlinearity in bonus contracts might even create incentives to decrease earnings (Murphy (1999)). It is often claimed that earnings management activities are especially prevalent before and after management changes. First of all a so-called "horizon problem" seems to exist, that is the departing manager may try to manipulate reported earnings (see Dechow and Sloan (1991) or Reitenga and Tearney (2003)). Yet, in addition a new manager might want to bias reported earnings directly after he or she has been hired which is referred to as the "big bath" (see for example Wells (2002) and Walsh (1991)).

In Chapter 5 we present a career concerns model which investigates factors that drive earnings management during managerial turnover. Our model is, to the best of our knowledge, the first to investigate the consequences of pre-announced managerial turnover on earnings management regarding both the departing and the incoming manager. Following the standard career concerns models we assume that the ability of both managers is unknown to all participants. Hence, all participants are uncertain about the talent of the managers and the market uses reported earnings to update its assessment of the managers ability or talent. Our model shows that both types of managers have incentives to bias reported earnings if they care about their reputation. While the departing manager brings earnings forward to his last period the new manager defers earnings from his early periods in the office to a later period in time. Moreover, higher bonus payments reduce the incentive to shift earnings for the new manager but increase them for the old one.

Chapter 2

Risk-Taking in Tournaments with Correlated Outcomes[1]

2.1 Introduction

In this chapter we study risk-taking in a simple tournament model where the outcomes of the risky strategy can be correlated. As in the real world the agents in our model make decisions which determine the variance of their outcome and these outcomes may be correlated.

Consider for instance two fund managers fighting for their clients' capital. While one of them has a good mid-year performance the other one is lagging behind. Another example is an election campaign with two politicians. Imagine one of them is a well-established front runner and the other one is fairly unknown. A key intuition often expressed in such settings is that a front runner should aim at safe options whereas a contestant trailing in the competition has incentives to choose a riskier strategy. However, if the assets (sets of policy options) from which the contestants can choose are very similar, it is harder for the underdog to differentiate from the favorite. The front runner may try to imitate a risky strategy chosen by his competitor exactly in order to protect his lead: independent of whether the assets rise or fall (the policy fails or succeeds with the voters) the relative position remains

---

[1]This chapter is based upon Nieken and Sliwka (2007).

unchanged if the strategy can be replicated exactly.

While previous tournament models deal with uncorrelated random terms (compare for example Lazear and Rosen (1981)) and ignore the possible connection between them, Taylor (2003) investigates the case with perfect correlation. He analyzes the behavior of mutual fund managers who can invest in portfolios which contain safe and risky assets. Both managers receive exactly the same return if they invest in the risky asset. In this game only a mixed equilibrium exists in which the leading agent chooses the riskier strategy more often than the trailing agent. However, in the real world options are often neither uncorrelated nor perfectly correlated. Therefore, we allow all possible correlations between zero and one. In a sense, our model nests Taylor's model with the more standard tournament models where the outcomes are uncorrelated.

There exists also empirical evidence about risk-taking in tournaments. As already pointed out for example Brown et al. (1996) or Chevalier and Ellison (1997) analyze the choice of risk of mutual fund managers. They show that mid-year losers (underperforming funds) increase total risk in contrast to outperforming funds. These findings are confirmed in general by several follow-up studies like Koski and Pontiff (1999) or Qui (2003) who reveals that top performing funds tend to "lock in" their position and funds close to them increase their risk. However, Busse (2001) contradicts these results using daily returns. He shows that mid-year winners increase their risk and losers decrease it during the second half of the year. Kempf et al. (forthcoming) deal with this contradicting findings by taking into account employment risk as well. They show that if employment risk is high mid-year losers tend to decrease risk relative to mid-year winners to secure their jobs. However, none of these papers takes into account the different correlations of the portfolios of fund managers because they cannot be observed in the field data.

Therefore, we develop a theoretical model dealing with different correlations and test its predictions in a controlled laboratory experiment. In our simple tournament model two contestants can choose between a safe or a risky option. We investigate under which circumstances a trailing agent indeed gambles and a front runner goes for the safe option. Our theoretical results depend strongly on the correlation between the outcomes of the risky strategies measuring the similarity between the set of actions available to the contestants. Additionally, the size of the lead of the front runner and the spread between winner and loser prize have impact on the equilibrium. There are three different equilibria possible. If the correlation is low the standard intuition that the leading agents prefer the safe option and the trailing agents choose the risky one indeed holds. This is no longer clear if the correlation is higher because the favorite will then switch to the risky strategy which leads to the equilibrium where both agents play risky. However, if the correlation is close to one only an equilibrium in mixed strategies exists.

The hypotheses derived from our theoretical model are tested in a controlled laboratory experiment. We use three treatments with different correlations. In the first treatment the correlation is zero while the second treatment deals with perfect correlation and the third treatment has a correlation of $\frac{1}{2}$. Each treatment consists of 23 rounds. Although we vary the size of the lead, indicating ability differences, in each round of each treatment we leave the spread between winner and loser prize unchanged during the whole experiment. Our experimental results are mostly in line with theory and show that whether the contestants prefer the safe or the risky strategy strongly depends on the correlation.

The remainder of this chapter is organized as follows. In Section 2.2 we introduce the model and analyze the possible Nash equilibria. Section 2.3 describes the experimental design and procedures. The hypotheses are shown in Section 2.4 and in Section 2.5 we present the experimental results. Section 2.6 concludes.

2.2 Theoretical Analysis

2.2.1 The Model

We consider a simple tournament between two agents A and B. We focus on the risk-taking decisions of the contestants and assume that both agents simultaneously decide among a risky and a safe strategy, i.e. $d_i \in \{r, s\}$ for

$i = A, B$. Each agent's decision affects the distribution of his performance y_i as:

$$y_i = \mu_s \qquad\qquad \text{if } d_i = s$$
$$y_i = \tilde{y}_i \sim N\left(\mu_r, \sigma^2\right) \quad \text{if } d_i = r$$

We allow for the possibility that one of the agents initially has a lead which may for instance be due to differences in ability or the outcome of some prior stage in the competition. Without loss of generality we assume that agent A has a lead and wins the tournament if the sum of his performance y_A and the lead Δy_A exceeds his rival's performance y_B where $\Delta y_A \geq 0$. When $y_A + \Delta y_A = y_B$ each agent wins the tournament with probability $\frac{1}{2}$.

Note that the variance of the risky option is the same for both agents. The performance outcomes $\tilde{y}_i$ are correlated with correlation coefficient ρ with $0 \leq \rho \leq 1$. Hence, we allow for the possibility that $\rho = 0$ as in Hvide (2002) and Kräkel and Sliwka (2004) or that $\rho = 1$ as in Taylor (2003) but also consider intermediate cases. The winner of the tournament receives a prize giving him an utility normalized to one and the loser's utility is zero. It is important to note that risk attitudes do not matter at all for the equilibrium outcomes as any rescaling of these two utility values does not alter the best responses.

2.2.2 Equilibrium Analysis

If both agents choose the safe option $d_A = d_B = s$ of course A always wins the tournament if Δy_A is strictly positive. For $\Delta y_A = 0$ each agent wins with probability $\frac{1}{2}$. When A plays safe agent B's only chance of winning is to choose the risky strategy. In this case A's winning probability is

$$P_A^{sr} = \Pr\{\Delta y_A + \mu_s\} > \tilde{y}_B = \Phi\left(\frac{\Delta y_A + \mu_s - \mu_r}{\sigma}\right)$$

where $\Phi\left(\cdot\right)$ is the cumulative distribution function of a standard normal distribution. If both agents choose the risky strategy player A wins with probability $P_A^{rr} = \Pr\{\tilde{y}_B - \tilde{y}_A\} < \Delta y_A$. Note that $\tilde{y}_B - \tilde{y}_A$ follows a normal distribution with mean 0 and variance $2\sigma^2 (1 - \rho)$. Hence,

$$
P_A^{rr} = \begin{cases} \Phi\left(\dfrac{\Delta y_A}{\sigma\sqrt{2(1-\rho)}}\right) & \text{if } 0 \leq \rho < 1 \\ 1 & \text{if } \rho = 1. \end{cases}
$$

Finally, when A plays risky and B plays safe, A's winning probability is

$$
P_A^{rs} = \Pr\{\Delta y_A + \tilde{y}_A\} > \mu_s = 1 - \Phi\left(\frac{\mu_s - \Delta y_A - \mu_r}{\sigma}\right).
$$

For ease of notation let $\Delta\mu = \mu_r - \mu_s$ which is positive if the risky strategy has a higher expected outcome than the safe one and negative in the opposite case. It is instructive to start with the case that $\Delta y_A = 0$. In this case the following simple game is played. The leading player A is the row and B is the column player.

	Risky	Safe
Risky	$\dfrac{1}{2}, \dfrac{1}{2}$	$\Phi\left(\frac{\Delta\mu}{\sigma}\right), \ \Phi\left(\frac{-\Delta\mu}{\sigma}\right)$
Safe	$\Phi\left(\frac{-\Delta\mu}{\sigma}\right), \ \Phi\left(\frac{\Delta\mu}{\sigma}\right)$	$\dfrac{1}{2}, \dfrac{1}{2}$

For $\Delta\mu = 0$ both players are indifferent between both strategies. But there is an unique Nash Equilibrium in dominant strategies in which both agents choose the risky strategy if the risky strategy has a higher return, i.e. $\Delta\mu > 0$. Whatever the opponent's strategy, a player can always raise the probability of winning by deviating to the risky strategy. If $\Delta\mu < 0$ the unique Nash Equilibrium in dominant strategies is (*safe, safe*).

Much more interesting is the case where one player has a lead, i.e. where w.l.o.g. $\Delta y_A > 0$. The agents then play the following zero sum game where again the leading player A is the row and player B the column player.

	Risky	Safe
Risky	$\Phi\left(\frac{\Delta y_A}{\sigma\sqrt{2(1-\rho)}}\right)$, $\Phi\left(\frac{-\Delta y_A}{\sigma\sqrt{2(1-\rho)}}\right)$	$\Phi\left(\frac{\Delta y_A+\Delta\mu}{\sigma}\right)$, $\Phi\left(\frac{-\Delta y_A-\Delta\mu}{\sigma}\right)$
Safe	$\Phi\left(\frac{\Delta y_A-\Delta\mu}{\sigma}\right)$, $\Phi\left(\frac{-\Delta y_A+\Delta\mu}{\sigma}\right)$	1, 0

First, it is straightforward to see that (*risky, safe*) and (*safe, safe*) can never be Nash Equilibria. In the first case, the leading player A wins for sure when deviating to the safe strategy. In the second, player B will always deviate to the risky strategy as he otherwise loses for sure.

If agent B plays risky the leading player A can indeed lose the tournament with a positive probability. It is interesting to investigate under what conditions he still prefers to stick to the safe strategy. He will prefer to do so if

$$\Phi\left(\frac{\Delta y_A}{\sigma\sqrt{2(1-\rho)}}\right) \leq \Phi\left(\frac{\Delta y_A-\Delta\mu}{\sigma}\right) \Leftrightarrow \frac{\Delta\mu}{\Delta y_A} \leq \left(1-\frac{1}{\sqrt{2(1-\rho)}}\right).$$

As playing risky leaves player B the only chance to win the tournament, we can directly conclude:

Proposition 1 *A pure strategy Nash Equilibrium exists in which the leading player A plays the safe strategy and player B plays the risky strategy if and only if*

$$\frac{\Delta\mu}{\Delta y_A} \leq 1 - \frac{1}{\sqrt{2(1-\rho)}}. \tag{2.1}$$

Hence, higher values of the lead Δy_A and smaller values of $\Delta\mu$ tend to make it more likely that the leading player sticks to the safe strategy. To understand the result it is instructive to consider first the case where the performance outcomes of the risky strategies are uncorrelated (i.e. $\rho = 0$). In this case,

16

Condition (2.1) is equivalent to $\frac{\Delta\mu}{\Delta y_A} \leq 1 - \frac{1}{2}\sqrt{2}$. If the risky strategy does not lead to a higher expected performance such that $\Delta\mu \leq 0$ the leading agent A will always stick to the safe strategy as playing the risky strategy will only raise the probability to forgo the leading position. The larger $\Delta\mu$ the more attractive it of course becomes to switch to the risky strategy. This will be the more so, the smaller the initial lead Δy_A as protecting a small lead is not worthwhile if the risky strategy becomes more attractive in terms of expected performance. Yet, it is interesting that this picture changes when the outcomes of the risky strategies are correlated. Note that Condition (2.1) is always violated if ρ tends to one.

The stronger the correlation between the risky strategies the more attractive it becomes for player A to choose the risky strategy if B has done the same – even if his lead Δy_A is large and even if the risky strategy does not lead to a much higher expected performance. The reason is that with correlated performance outcomes, choosing the risky strategy becomes a means to protect the lead. Hence, we now have to check under which conditions a Nash Equilibrium exists in which both agents play the risky strategy.

As analyzed above, when B plays risky the leading player A will prefer to play risky as well if Condition (2.1) is violated, i.e.

$$\frac{\Delta\mu}{\Delta y_A} > \left(1 - \frac{1}{\sqrt{2(1-\rho)}}\right). \tag{2.2}$$

Player B then indeed also prefers the risky option if

$$\Phi\left(\frac{-\Delta y_A}{\sigma\sqrt{2(1-\rho)}}\right) \geq \Phi\left(\frac{-\Delta y_A - \Delta\mu}{\sigma}\right)$$

$$\Leftrightarrow \frac{\Delta\mu}{\Delta y_A} \geq \left(\frac{1}{\sqrt{2(1-\rho)}} - 1\right). \tag{2.3}$$

Hence, we can conclude.[2]

---

[2]Note that $(safe, risky)$ and $(risky, risky)$ both exist if $\frac{\Delta\mu}{\Delta y_A} = \left(1 - \frac{1}{\sqrt{2(1-\rho)}}\right)$.

Proposition 2 *A pure strategy Nash Equilibrium exists in which both play-ers choose the risky strategy if and only if*

$$\frac{\Delta\mu}{\Delta y_A} \geq \max\left\{1 - \frac{1}{\sqrt{2\left(1-\rho\right)}}, \frac{1}{\sqrt{2\left(1-\rho\right)}} - 1\right\}. \qquad (2.4)$$

Note that Condition (2.4) is always violated if $\Delta\mu \leq 0$. If the risky strategy does not lead to a higher expected outcome than the safe one the players will never play (*risky, risky*).

For $\Delta\mu > 0$ first consider again the case where the outcomes of the risky strategies are uncorrelated (i.e. $\rho = 0$). Condition (2.4) is now equivalent to $\frac{\Delta\mu}{\Delta y_A} \geq 1 - \frac{1}{2}\sqrt{2}$. Note that this is the opposite of Condition (2.1) given in Proposition 1. The reason is that player B always prefers the risky strategy if $\rho = 0$ irrespective of A's decision. As already laid out, if A plays safe playing the risky strategy is the only way for player B to have at least a chance of winning. When, however, A plays risky, player B has such a chance already when playing safe, but can increase the odds by choosing risky. Hence, for $\rho = 0$ only player A's considerations determine which equilibrium is played. Both play risky in this case if and only if $\frac{\Delta\mu}{\Delta y_A}$ is sufficiently large as only then it will be reasonable for player A to take the risk and not to protect the lead. As pointed out above, the reasoning is different if the outcomes of the risky strategies are correlated. As we have already seen, agent A has an incentive to imitate the risky strategy of his opponent if the correlation gets stronger. To see this consider Figure 2.1, in which the equilibrium conditions are mapped in the $\left(\rho, \frac{\Delta\mu}{\Delta y_A}\right)$-space. Condition (2.2) determines the downward sloping curve which separates the region in which agent A plays safe and agent B plays risky from that where both choose risky. The higher ρ the more attractive it becomes for agent A to switch to the risky strategy as well. A special case is $\rho = \frac{1}{2}$. In this case Condition (2.4) simplifies to $\frac{\Delta\mu}{\Delta y_A} \geq 0$ and, hence, the agents will always play (*risky, risky*) whenever $\Delta\mu \geq 0$ no matter how large the initial lead is.

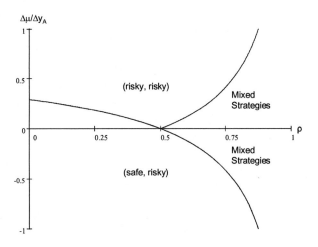

Figure 2.1: Nash Equilibria of the game

But when the correlation gets stronger, choosing the risky strategy becomes less attractive for player B. The stronger the correlation the smaller is the probability for player B to overtake player A if both play risky. In the extreme, if $\rho = 1$, both agents will always attain the same outcome when playing the risky strategy and, hence, agent A would win for sure. In that case, however, player B has an incentive to deviate to the safe strategy if player A chooses risky. Playing safe leaves at least the possibility that A is unlucky and falls behind. Yet of course, if player A in turn knows that B chooses the safe strategy, he would again want to deviate and choose the safe strategy as well. Hence, we cannot have equilibria in pure strategies if $\rho = 1$ as has been shown by Taylor (2003). Note that we can already conclude from Propositions 1 and 2 that a similar reasoning must hold for a larger set of parameters. As we have previously checked the existence conditions for all potential pure strategy equilibria, if Conditions (2.1) and (2.4) are both violated only mixed strategy equilibria can exist. This leads to the following result.

Proposition 3 *A Nash Equilibrium in mixed strategies exists if and only if*

$$1 - \frac{1}{\sqrt{2(1-\rho)}} < \frac{\Delta\mu}{\Delta y_A} < \frac{1}{\sqrt{2(1-\rho)}} - 1. \tag{2.5}$$

In any mixed strategy equilibrium, player A chooses the risky strategy with a higher probability than player B if the risky strategy leads to a higher expected outcome than the safe one. If $\Delta\mu < 0$ player B chooses the risky strategy with a higher probability than his opponent. Both players choose the risky strategy with equal probability if $\Delta\mu = 0$.

Proof: See Appendix.

Hence, only mixed strategy equilibria exist in the area between the two curves in Figure 2.1 if $\rho > \frac{1}{2}$. The larger the correlation between the outcomes of the risky strategies and the smaller the absolute value of $\frac{\Delta\mu}{\Delta y_A}$ the more likely it is that a mixed strategy is played. In such an equilibrium, the leading player always chooses the risky strategy with a higher probability than his opponent if $\Delta\mu > 0$. In this case, the higher expected payoff of the risky strategy makes it more attractive to gamble and the leading player can afford to gamble with a higher probability due to his lead. If the outcome of the safe strategy is equal to the expected outcome of the risky strategy both players will choose the risky strategy with equal probability. The trailing player chooses the risky strategy with a higher probability than the leading one if $\Delta\mu < 0$. Here, the trailing player has a stronger incentive to play risky although this entails a loss in expected payoffs.

2.3 Experimental Design and Procedure

We implemented the simple risk-taking tournament in a controlled laboratory experiment. The experiment consisted of three different treatments testing the behavior of the players in tournament situations with different correlations. Each treatment contained one session with 24 participants who played 23 rounds. Hence, we collected 552 observations for each treatment.

In each of the 23 rounds two players were matched together randomly and anonymously. Therefore, each participant played 23 times and each time with a different opponent. This perfect stranger matching was implemented to prevent reputation effects. We varied the correlation coefficient of the risky strategy between the treatments. The first treatment had a correlation coefficient of zero, the second of one and the third of $\frac{1}{2}$. Furthermore, we varied the lead Δy_A between the rounds such that we were able to investigate the effects of Δy_A on players strategy choices.

The experiment was conducted at the Cologne Laboratory of Economic Research at the University of Cologne in January 2007. Altogether 72 students participated in the experiment. All of them were enrolled in the Faculty of Management, Economics, and Social Sciences and had completed their second year of studies. For the recruitment of the participants we used the online recruitment system by Greiner (2003). We used the experimental software z-tree by Fischbacher (2007) for programming the experiment.

At the outset of each session the subjects were randomly assigned to a cubicle where they took a seat in front of a computer terminal. The instructions were handed out and read out by the experimenters.[3] After this the subjects had time to pose questions if they had any difficulties in understanding the instructions. Communication - other than with the experimental software - was not allowed.

Each session started with five trial rounds so that the players became familiar with the game. In this trial rounds each player had the opportunity to simulate the game by choosing the strategies for both players and observing the outcomes. After this the 23 main rounds started. All rounds were identical but played with a different partner. At the beginning of each round the players were informed about their score of points which they had in the beginning and the score of their opponent. So they knew whether they were the player in lead and how large the difference between the scores was. The initial scores of points were drawn from a normal distribution with a mean of 150 points and a standard deviation of 42 points. After learning about

---

[3] The full set of the experimental instructions translated into English can be found in the Appendix.

the initial scores the players had to decide whether they wanted to play a safe or a risky strategy. If a player chose the safe strategy he received 80 additional points for sure. When choosing the risky strategy the additional points awarded were determined by a random draw from a normal distribution with a mean of 100 points and a standard deviation of 20 points. In the first treatment the risky strategies of both players were uncorrelated. In the second treatment the risky strategies were perfectly correlated and in the third they were correlated with $\rho = \frac{1}{2}$. This information was common knowledge. The key concepts were explained in the instructions and the players had the opportunity to develop a "feeling" for the distribution in the trial rounds. After each player had made his decision they were informed about the additional points received and the final score of the game. The final score was the sum of the initial points of each player and his additional points won in the game. They were also informed which player was the winner of the round. After this a new round with a different partner started. At the end of the experiment one of the 23 rounds was drawn by lot. Each player who won the tournament in which he participated in the drawn round earned 25 Euro each loser earned 5 Euro. Additionally, all subjects received a show up fee of 2.50 Euro independent of their status as winner or loser. On average the players earned 17.50 Euro. After the last round the subjects were requested to complete a questionnaire including questions on gender, age and risk attitude. The questions concerning the risk attitude were taken from the German Socio Economic Panel (GSOEP) and deal with the overall risk attitude of the subject. Dohmen et al. (2005) have shown that the general question about the willingness to take risks is a good predictor of actual risk-taking behavior and the risk choice in lotteries. The whole procedure took about one hour.

2.4 Hypotheses

First of all, based on the theoretical reasoning above, we expect that in the treatment without correlation the leader plays the safe strategy more often than the trailing player (Hypothesis 1). But of course, the model makes a more precise prediction. Recall that the trailing player should always choose the risky strategy. The leader should play the safe strategy if and only if the lead is sufficiently large and the expected gains from playing risky are low. In our experiment the expected gains from playing risky are fixed for all treatments ($\Delta\mu = 20$). In other words the player in lead should choose the safe strategy if $\Delta y_A > \frac{20}{1-\frac{1}{2}\sqrt{2}} = 68.28$ and otherwise should prefer the risky strategy.

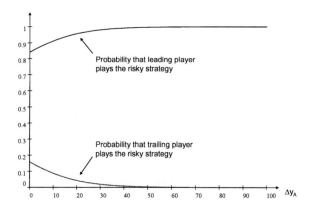

Figure 2.2: Equilibrium mixed strategies if rho=1

In the second treatment the performance outcomes of the risky strategies are perfectly correlated and therefore only an equilibrium in mixed strategies exists in the theoretical model. But the most important and testable implication is that – in contrast to the zero correlation case – we expect that the player in lead will play risky more often than his opponent (Hypothesis 2). Although we cannot expect that the participants in the experiment are able to coordinate on the mixed strategies equilibrium perfectly, the data should at least be in line with some qualitative features of the equilibrium. Therefore, it is useful to consider the probabilities with which the players choose the risky strategy derived in the proof of Proposition 3. Figure 2.2 shows these probabilities as a function of Δy_A for the parameter values used in the experiment. Note that the leading player should choose the risky strategy in

23

more than 80% and the trailing player in less than 20% of the cases. Further-more, we expect that the probability that the trailing player plays the risky strategy should decrease in Δy_A and the probability that the leader does the same should increase in his lead.

For the third treatment we predict that both players will always choose the risky option no matter how large the lead is (Hypothesis 3) or at least that they both learn during the course of the experiment that the risky strategy is beneficial.

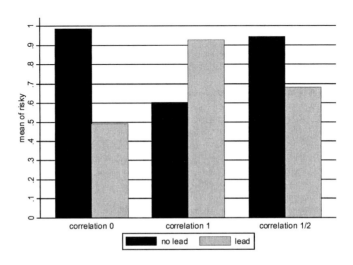

Figure 2.3: Choice of risk for each treatment

2.5 Results

We now test these hypotheses with the data from our experiment. Figure 2.3 shows the fraction of rounds in which the players in each treatment choose the risky strategy depending on whether the player has a lead or not.[4] We start by investigating the results from treatment 1 where the outcomes of the risky

---

[4]Table 2.4 in the Appendix gives the precise values. Note that the mean of risky is equal to the fraction of rounds the players prefer the risky strategy.

strategies are uncorrelated. Looking at Figure 2.3 we already see that the trailing player almost always chooses the risky strategy if the risky strategies are uncorrelated but that the leading player chooses the safe strategy in nearly 50% of the cases. Hence, these observations are well in line with Hypothesis 1. To analyze whether the lead has an effect on the choice of strategy for the leader we run probit regressions. The dependent variable is the probability that the leading agent chooses the risky strategy. As one subject plays the game 23 times we report robust standard errors clustered by subjects.[5] The results are reported in Table 2.1.[6]

	(1) Leading player	(2) Leading player
Lead	−0.0284***	
	(0.0043)	
Lead > 68.28		−1.3990***
		(0.2200)
Round	0.0059	0.0052
	(0.0120)	(0.0095)
Constant	1.1920***	0.2440
	(0.2200)	(0.1900)
Observations	276	276
Pseudo Loglikelihood	−136.62092	−163.80531
Pseudo R^2	0.2858	0.1436

Robust standard errors in parentheses are calculated by clustering on subjects
***$p < 0.01$, **$p < 0.05$, *$p < 0.10$

Table 2.1: Probit regressions for leading players in treatment 1

The variable round is included to check for time trends capturing possible learning effects. We see from column (1) that in line with the theoretical

---

[5] As an alternative we run random effects regressions. The results remain qualitatively unchanged and are reported in Table 2.6 in the Appendix.

[6] In the Appendix we report the marginal effects for all probit regressions.

prediction, a larger lead makes it indeed more likely for the leader to choose the safe strategy. This effect is highly significant. Regression (2) uses a dummy variable which takes value one if the lead is larger than 68.28 and zero otherwise. The results are qualitatively similar to those reported in regression (1). Note that there are no significant time trends. Furthermore, we tested whether the risk attitude of the players has an impact on their decision. In line with theory our results show no significant influence of the risk attitude on the behavior of the players. Compare Table 2.7 in the Appendix.

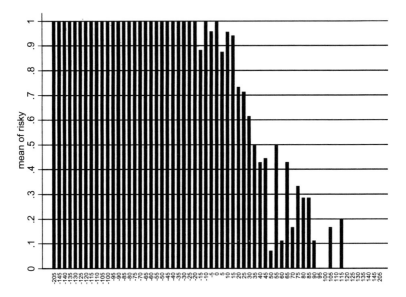

Figure 2.4: Choice of the risky strategy for different leads in treatment 1

Of course, the participants do not switch to the safe strategy precisely at the predicted cut-off value, but still they learn surprisingly well that playing safe is preferable if the lead gets larger as is also illustrated in Figure 2.4. It shows the fractions of the risky strategy choice of the leading and the trailing agents for different leads in treatment 1 (interval size five). We can summarize these observations as follows.

26

Result 1 ($\rho = 0$): *If the outcomes of the risky strategies are uncorrelated the leading players choose the safe strategy more often than their opponents. The trailing players nearly always choose the risky strategy (98.9%). The size of the lead has a strong influence on the probability that the leader chooses the safe strategy: The larger the lead, the more often the safe strategy is chosen.*

We now turn to the perfect correlation case in treatment 2. A look at Figure 2.3 already indicates that the leading player picks the risky option more often than his opponent which is in stark contrast to the results from treatment 1 but well in line with the theoretical prediction for treatment 2.

	(1)	(2)
	Leading player	Trailing player
Lead	−0.0054*	0.0094***
	(0.0031)	(0.0035)
Round	0.0775***	−0.0332***
	(0.0160)	(0.0110)
Constant	0.9760***	0.2460
	(0.2100)	(0.1900)
Observations	276	276
Pseudo Loglikelihood	−63.41759	−173.62979
Pseudo R^2	0.1161	0.0623

Robust standard errors in parentheses are calculated by clustering on subjects
***$p < 0.01$, **$p < 0.05$, *$p < 0.10$

Table 2.2: Probit regressions for treatment 2

Furthermore, as the theory predicts the leading players choose the risky strategy in more than 80% (92.8%) of the cases. But the trailing players also choose the risky option in 60.5% of the cases and not as we predicted in less than 20% of the cases. This behavior may be due to the false intuition that they have nothing to lose and therefore they prefer to gamble. The trailing players seem to disregard at least partially that the leader may also want to play the risky strategy in which case the best reply is to play safe as only this leaves a chance to win the tournament. Again, we run probit regressions to test the predictions of the model.[7] We first consider the leading players' behavior in regression (1) and then that of the trailing players in regression (2) of Table 2.2. First, note that we have to reject our prediction concerning the effect of the lead in both cases. The theoretical model predicts that the leader plays the risky strategy more often the larger the lead and the trailing player plays risky less often for larger initial differences. The empirical analysis shows the opposite signs for both effects. It seems that initially the players follow the much more straightforward intuition from the case where the outcomes are uncorrelated, i.e. that the leader should protect his lead by playing safe and the trailing player can only "attack" the leader by choosing the risky strategy. But note that we observe strong learning effects that seem to direct the players closer to the equilibrium prediction. Over the course of the experiment the leading players significantly increase the frequency of playing the risky strategy and the trailing players reduce this frequency.[8] We can summarize:

Result 2 ($\rho = 1$): *If the outcomes of the risky strategies are perfectly correlated the leading players choose the risky strategy more often than their opponents. The leaders choose the risky strategy in 92.8% and the trailing players in 60.5% of the cases. Over the course of the experiment the leading players increase the frequency of playing the risky strategy, whereas the trailing players reduce this frequency.*

Finally, we consider the results from the third treatment in which the correlation coefficient between the outcomes of the risky strategies is $\rho = \frac{1}{2}$. According to our theoretical predictions both players should always play the risky strategy regardless how large the lead is. As we see in Figure 2.3 this prediction is true only for the trailing players. Leading agents choose the

---

[7] Again, we also run random effects regressions and regressions controlling for risk attitude. The results remain qualitativly the same and the risk attitude has no significant influence on the decision of the players. See Tables 2.9 and 2.10 in the Appendix for the complete results.

[8] Compare Figure 2.5 in the Appendix for a graphical overview.

risky option only in 68.1% of the cases. To analyze learning effects and the effect of the lead on the choice of the strategy we again use a probit regression with the choice of strategy as dependent variable. The results of the regression are reported in Table 2.3.[9]

	Leading player
Lead	−0.0139***
	(0.0034)
Round	0.0263***
	(0.0094)
Constant	0.8070***
	(0.2000)
Observations	276
Pseudo Loglikelihood	−153.97572
Pseudo R^2	0.1088

Robust standard errors in parentheses are calculated by clustering on subjects
***$p < 0.01$, **$p < 0.05$, *$p < 0.10$

Table 2.3: Probit regression for leading players in treatment 3

The regression shows that the lead indeed has an effect on the choice of the strategy. The probability that the leader plays the safe option rises if the lead gets larger. This effect might occur because the leader thinks that playing safe is an appropriate way to protect his leading position. During the experiment the leader learns that this assumption is not true and chooses the risky strategy more often. When we take a look at the decisions the leading players make in the last five rounds, we see that 76.7% of them prefer the risky strategy. This leads to the following result.

Result 3 ($\rho = \frac{1}{2}$): *If the outcomes of the risky strategies are correlated with* $\rho = \frac{1}{2}$ *the trailing players play the risky strategy in nearly all cases* (94.6%). *The leading players choose the risky strategy in only* 68.1% *of the cases but*

---

[9]The results of the random effects regression and the regression controlling for risk attitude can be found in Tables 2.12 and 2.13 in the Appendix.

increase this frequency over the course of the experiment.

Hence, it seems to be the case that learning directs the players towards the equilibrium prediction.

2.6 Conclusion

We have investigated a simple tournament model in which two agents simultaneously choose between a risky and a safe strategy. Our analysis shows that the equilibrium outcome strongly depends on the correlation between the outcomes of the risky strategy. We then tested the predictions made based on the model in a controlled laboratory experiment. The key predictions have been confirmed: The leading players choose the safe strategy more often than the trailing players if the outcomes are uncorrelated, but the contrary is true if the outcomes are perfectly correlated.

From a more general standpoint, our model as well as the empirical results cast some light on the attractiveness of gambling in competitive situations. One interpretation of the correlation between the risky strategies is the similarity in the set of available policy options. If the competitors have access to similar policies, the correlation between the outcomes of the risky strategies will be high. In this case, a trailing contestant can no longer be certain that his opponent will stick to the safe strategy when choosing to gamble. It even has turned out that the leading player will have a stronger incentive to gamble than his trailing opponent if the risky strategy has higher rewards in expected terms.

There are many open questions for future research. For instance, we so far do not consider endogenous effort choices and focus only on risk-taking behavior. Moreover, it would be interesting to study risk-taking behavior in dynamic tournaments where the agents can react to past choices of their opponents, for instance, to cast more light on the timing of risk-taking decisions in competitive environments.

2.7 Appendix to Chapter 2

Proof of Proposition 3:

Both players will randomize only if they are indifferent between the payoffs of both strategies. Suppose that player A chooses the risky strategy with probability p and player B with probability q. Hence, we must have that

$$p \cdot \Phi \left(\frac{-\Delta y_A}{\sigma \sqrt{2(1-\rho)}} \right) + (1-p) \cdot \Phi \left(\frac{-\Delta y_A + \Delta \mu}{\sigma} \right) = p \cdot \Phi \left(\frac{-\Delta y_A - \Delta \mu}{\sigma} \right) + (1-p) \cdot 0 \Leftrightarrow$$

$$p = \frac{\Phi \left(\frac{-\Delta y_A + \Delta \mu}{\sigma} \right)}{\Phi \left(\frac{-\Delta y_A + \Delta \mu}{\sigma} \right) + \Phi \left(\frac{-\Delta y_A - \Delta \mu}{\sigma} \right) - \Phi \left(\frac{-\Delta y_A}{\sigma \sqrt{2(1-\rho)}} \right)}$$

and

$$q \cdot \Phi \left(\frac{\Delta y_A}{\sigma \sqrt{2(1-\rho)}} \right) + (1-q) \cdot \Phi \left(\frac{\Delta y_A + \Delta \mu}{\sigma} \right) = q \cdot \Phi \left(\frac{\Delta y_A - \Delta \mu}{\sigma} \right) + (1-q) \cdot 1 \Leftrightarrow$$

$$q = \frac{1 - \Phi \left(\frac{\Delta y_A + \Delta \mu}{\sigma} \right)}{1 + \Phi \left(\frac{\Delta y_A}{\sigma \sqrt{2(1-\rho)}} \right) - \Phi \left(\frac{\Delta y_A + \Delta \mu}{\sigma} \right) - \Phi \left(\frac{\Delta y_A - \Delta \mu}{\sigma} \right)}.$$

Player A will indeed choose the risky strategy with higher probability than player B if

$$\frac{\Phi \left(\frac{-\Delta y_A + \Delta \mu}{\sigma} \right)}{\Phi \left(\frac{-\Delta y_A + \Delta \mu}{\sigma} \right) + \Phi \left(\frac{-\Delta y_A - \Delta \mu}{\sigma} \right) - \Phi \left(\frac{-\Delta y_A}{\sigma \sqrt{2(1-\rho)}} \right)}$$

$$> \frac{1 - \Phi \left(\frac{\Delta y_A + \Delta \mu}{\sigma} \right)}{1 + \Phi \left(\frac{\Delta y_A}{\sigma \sqrt{2(1-\rho)}} \right) - \Phi \left(\frac{\Delta y_A + \Delta \mu}{\sigma} \right) - \Phi \left(\frac{\Delta y_A - \Delta \mu}{\sigma} \right)}$$

using that $\Phi(x) = 1 - \Phi(-x)$ this is equivalent to

$$\frac{\Phi\left(\frac{-\Delta y_A + \Delta \mu}{\sigma}\right)}{1 + \Phi\left(\frac{\Delta y_A}{\sigma\sqrt{2(1-\rho)}}\right) - \Phi\left(\frac{\Delta y_A - \Delta \mu}{\sigma}\right) - \Phi\left(\frac{\Delta y_A + \Delta \mu}{\sigma}\right)}$$

$$> \frac{1 - \Phi\left(\frac{\Delta y_A + \Delta \mu}{\sigma}\right)}{1 + \Phi\left(\frac{\Delta y_A}{\sigma\sqrt{2(1-\rho)}}\right) - \Phi\left(\frac{\Delta y_A + \Delta \mu}{\sigma}\right) - \Phi\left(\frac{\Delta y_A - \Delta \mu}{\sigma}\right)}$$

$$\Leftrightarrow \quad \Phi\left(\frac{-\Delta y_A + \Delta \mu}{\sigma}\right) > 1 - \Phi\left(\frac{\Delta y_A + \Delta \mu}{\sigma}\right)$$

$$\Leftrightarrow \quad \Phi\left(\frac{-\Delta y_A + \Delta \mu}{\sigma}\right) > \Phi\left(\frac{-\Delta y_A - \Delta \mu}{\sigma}\right)$$

which is true if $\Delta \mu > 0$. In the special case $\Delta \mu = 0$ both players choose the risky strategy with equal probability. If $\Delta \mu < 0$ Player B will choose the risky strategy with a higher probability than player A. $\blacksquare$

	Correlation 0		Correlation 1		Correlation $\frac{1}{2}$	
	no lead	lead	no lead	lead	no lead	lead
Safe	0.011	0.507	0.395	0.072	0.054	0.319
Risky	0.989	0.493	0.605	0.928	0.946	0.681

Table 2.4: Distribution of strategy choices for all treatments

	(1) Leading player	(2) Leading player
Lead	−0.0113***	
	(0.0016)	
Lead > 68.28		−0.4830***
		(0.0620)
Round	0.0023	0.0021
	(0.0046)	(0.0038)
Observations	276	276
Pseudo Loglikelihood	−136.62092	−163.80531
Pseudo R^2	0.2858	0.1436

Robust standard errors in parentheses are calculated by clustering on subjects
Marginal effects reported, ***$p < 0.01$, **$p < 0.05$, *$p < 0.10$

Table 2.5: Probit regressions for leading players in treatment 1, marginal effects reported

	(1) Leading player	(2) Leading player
Lead	−0.0453*** (0.0057)	
Lead > 68.28		−1.8520*** (0.2600)
Round	0.0059 (0.0170)	0.0079 (0.0140)
Constant	1.9620*** (0.4300)	0.3340 (0.2500)
Observations	276	276
Log Likelihood	−110.38209	−147.50784

Random effects estimation, standard errors in parentheses
***$p < 0.01$, **$p < 0.05$, *$p < 0.10$

Table 2.6: Probit regressions with random effects for leading players in treatment 1

	(1) Leading player	(2) Leading player
Lead	−0.0285*** (0.0043)	
Lead > 68.28		−1.4050*** (0.2200)
Round	0.0060 (0.0110)	0.0056 (0.0092)
Risk attitude	−0.0046 (0.0610)	−0.0141 (0.0520)
Constant	1.2140*** (0.4000)	0.3120 (0.3500)
Observations	276	276
Pseudo Loglikelihood	−136.61206	−163.70813
Pseudo R^2	0.2858	0.1441

Robust standard errors in parentheses are calculated by clustering on subjects,
***$p < 0.01$, **$p < 0.05$, *$p < 0.10$

Table 2.7: Probit regressions for leading players in treatment 1 controlling for risk attitude

	(1)	(2)
	Leading player	Trailing player
Lead	−0.000545*	0.003610***
	(0.00041)	(0.00130)
Round	0.007830***	−0.012700***
	(0.00270)	(0.00430)
Observations	276	276
Pseudo Loglikelihood	−63.41759	−173.62979
Pseudo R^2	0.1161	0.0623

Robust standard errors in parentheses are calculated by clustering on subjects
Marginal effects reported, ***$p < 0.01$, **$p < 0.05$, *$p < 0.10$

Table 2.8: Probit regressions for treatment 2, marginal effects reported

	(1)	(2)
	Leading player	Trailing player
Lead	−0.0067	0.0140***
	(0.0047)	(0.0029)
Round	0.0927***	−0.0501***
	(0.0270)	(0.0140)
Constant	1.4060***	0.3610
	(0.4500)	(0.2900)
Observations	276	276
Log Likelihood	−56.69389	−151.31980

Random effects estimation, standard errors in parentheses
***$p < 0.01$, **$p < 0.05$, *$p < 0.10$

Table 2.9: Probit regressions with random effects for treatment 2

	(1)	(2)
	Leading player	Trailing player
Lead	−0.00538*	0.00954***
	(0.0032)	(0.0034)
Round	0.07720***	−0.03410***
	(0.0160)	(0.0110)
Risk attitude	−0.03930	0.04850
	(0.0810)	(0.0780)
Constant	1.21000**	−0.01070
	(0.5300)	(0.5000)
Observations	276	276
Pseudo Loglikelihood	−63.16817	−173.62979
Pseudo R^2	0.1196	0.0623

Robust standard errors in parentheses are calculated by clustering on subjects
$p < 0.01$, **$p < 0.05$, *$p < 0.10$

Table 2.10: Probit regressions for treatment 2 controlling for risk attitude

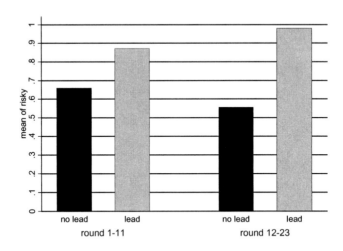

Figure 2.5: Choice of risk in treatment 2

	Leading player
Lead	−0.00483***
	(0.0015)
Round	0.00918***
	(0.0033)
Observations	276
Pseudo Loglikelihood	−153.97572
Pseudo R^2	0.1088

Robust standard errors in parentheses are calculated by clustering on subjects

Marginal effects reported, ***$p < 0.01$, **$p < 0.05$, *$p < 0.10$

Table 2.11: Probit regression for leading players in treatment 3, marginal effects reported

	Leading player
Lead	−0.0252***
	(0.0043)
Round	0.0460***
	(0.0170)
Constant	1.2860***
	(0.4000)
Observations	276
Log Likelihood	−117.24643

Random effects estimation, standard errors in parentheses

***$p < 0.01$, **$p < 0.05$, *$p < 0.10$

Table 2.12: Probit regression with random effects for leading players in treatment 3

	Leading player
Lead	−0.0140***
	(0.0035)
Round	0.0272***
	(0.0095)
Risk attitude	0.0750
	(0.0790)
Constant	0.4010
	(0.4700)
Observations	276
Pseudo Loglikelihood	−152.39838
Pseudo R^2	0.1179

Robust standard errors in parentheses are calculated by clustering on subjects

***$p < 0.01$, **$p < 0.05$, *$p < 0.10$

Table 2.13: Probit regression for leading players in treatment 3 controlling for risk attitude

Instructions for the experiment

(Note that the instructions had to be slightly different for each treatment. The parts that are only valid for one of the treatments are marked with (treatment 1), (treatment 2) or (treatment 3) here.)

Welcome to this experiment!

Please read these instructions carefully. If you have any questions please raise your hand and ask us. Please note the following:

- There is no communication allowed.

- All decisions are anonymous. None of the other participants will learn the identity of the one who makes a certain decision.

- The payment is anonymous, too. Nobody gets to know how high the payment of another participant is.

- This experiment consists of two parts. The first part will be explained now. The second part consists only of a short questionnaire.

Rounds and Partners

- The experiment consists of 23 rounds.

- Before the experiment starts you will have the chance to get a better feeling for it in five trial rounds. These trial rounds have no influence on your payment. Their only purpose is to help you develop a better understanding of the experiment.

- You will play each round with a different partner. The identity of your partner will not be revealed. We have ensured that you will never play with the same partner again.

Progress of one round

- At the beginning of each round you will be matched with one partner.

- At the start of each round you will learn your own score and that of your partner. With this information you can infer whether you have a lead or are lagging behind your partner. The initial scores are determined randomly.

- You have to decide between two strategies. Strategy A will give you 80 additional points for sure. Strategy B will give you additional points that are determined by a random draw from a normal distribution with a mean of 100 points and a standard deviation of 20 points. You will find a chart at the end of this instruction to clarify this distribution.

- Your partner can also choose between strategy A and B. There are four possible outcomes:

   - both players choose strategy A.
   - you choose strategy A and your partner chooses strategy B.
   - you choose strategy B and your partner chooses strategy A.
   - both players choose strategy B.

- (treatment 1) If both players choose strategy B with the random return you have to keep in mind that the outcomes are completely independent of each other. If you achieve a certain amount of additional points by choosing the strategy with the random return the additional points your partner achieves when also playing the strategy with the random return are completely independent of your points.

- (treatment 2) If both players choose strategy B with the random return you have to keep in mind that the outcomes are perfectly correlated. If you achieve a certain amount of additional points by choosing the strategy with the random return your partner will always achieve the same amount of additional points if he chooses this strategy as well.

- (treatment 3) If both players choose strategy B with the random return you have to keep in mind that the outcomes are correlated, i.e. there is a relation between the outcomes. The correlation coefficient in this experiment is 0.5. It is a measure for the relationship between the points score of both players. If you play the strategy with the random return and achieve a high additional point score the probability is high that your partner will also attain a high score when playing this strategy as well. If you play the strategy with the random return and achieve a rather low additional point score the probability is high that your partner will also attain only a low score if he is also playing this strategy. We will give you more information about the correlation coefficient at the end this instruction.

- After both players have made their decision about the strategy the results of the round will be calculated. The final result is the sum of the initial points and the additional point score you attained in this game. If your final score is higher than that of your partner you are the winner of this round. If your final score is smaller than that of your partner you have lost this round. If the scores are equal the winner will be drawn by lot.

- After you and your partner have been informed about your final scores and the winner of the round you will be matched with a new partner. Then the game starts again.

- You will play 23 rounds with different partners. Please note that you will only play once with a certain partner.

- After the 23 rounds one round is drawn by lot which determines your payment. If you are the winner of that round you will receive the winner prize of 25 Euro. If you have lost this round you will receive the loser prize of five Euro.

- The second part of the experiment starts. Please fill out the questionnaire which will appear on the screen.

- Please stay at your seat until we call your cubicle number. Please bring along this instruction and your cubicle number. Otherwise we cannot hand out the payment.

> Your payment as winner =
> Winner prize 25 Euro + 2.50 Euro show-up fee
> = 27.50 Euro
>
> Your payment as loser =
> Loser prize 5 Euro + 2.50 Euro show-up fee
> = 7.50 Euro

Thank you for participation and good luck!

Additional comments:

Strategy B

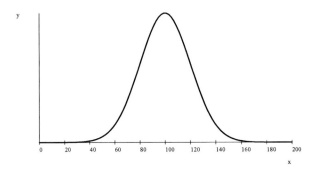

Figure 2.6: Chart of the normal distribution with a mean of 100 and a standard deviation of 20

Reminder:

The probability that the additional point score belongs to a certain interval corresponds to the size of the surface under the graph. For instance, 95.44% of the drawn points are located in the interval between 60 and 140.

(treatment 3)

Explanation of correlation:

The correlation coefficient is a measure for the linear relationship between two random variables. It can vary between -1 and 1. If it is 1 there is a perfect positive linear relationship between the random numbers. Graphically the scatterplot follows a straight line. If the correlation coefficient is zero the random numbers are independent from each other. In this experiment the correlation coefficient is 0.5.

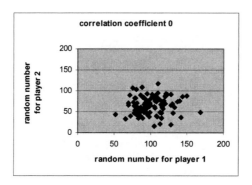

Figure 2.7: Correlation coefficient of zero

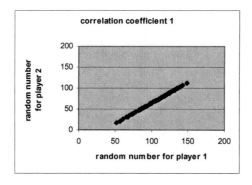

Figure 2.8: Correlation coefficient of one

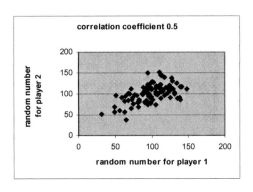

Figure 2.9: Correlation coefficient of 0.5

Chapter 3

Risk-Taking and Effort in Tournaments with Homogeneous Agents[1]

3.1 Introduction

The purpose of this chapter is to investigate risk-taking and the choice of effort in a two-stage tournament model empirically. In the real world agents often first select risk before they decide about their effort to win the tournament. For example, managers may have the option to implement a new and often more risky technology or to stick to the old, standard one before they decide about their effort. We derive several hypotheses concerning risk-taking and effort based on the models developed by Hvide (2002) and Kräkel and Sliwka (2004) which are tested in a controlled laboratory experiment.

Hvide (2002) and Kräkel and Sliwka (2004) both investigate two-stage tournaments with the choice of risk at the first stage and the effort decision at the second stage. In his paper Hvide (2002) analyzes a tournament with homogeneous agents. He shows that agents -if possible- prefer infinite risk at the first stage which leads to zero effort at the second stage. He offers a solution called k-contracts to prevent this kind of behavior in tournaments.

---

[1]This chapter is based on Nieken (2008).

In this kind of reward scheme agents are not paid according to their relative performance but according to the relative closeness of their output to a benchmark k. This scheme should avoid excessive risk-taking and induce incentives to work. In contrast Kräkel and Sliwka (2004) investigate risk-taking of heterogeneous agents. In their setting risk is limited and the agents can either choose a high or a low risk. In this model the choice of risk at the first stage affects equilibrium efforts and the winning probability as well which leads to diverse equilibria.

In our design we focus on homogeneous agents and are able to observe the agents' choice of risk in the first stage and their effort decision in the second stage. Hence, we can (*i*) investigate the risk-taking behavior of the agents and (*ii*) analyze their effort reactions towards different states of risk. Thereby we are able to check the central predictions of the risk-taking strand of the tournament literature.

In our experiment the agents can choose between two levels of risk before they have to decide about their effort. In contrast to the previous chapter the outcomes of the risky strategies are uncorrelated as in the classical tournament models. We also elicit the players' beliefs about the effort choice of their opponents before they decide about their own effort level. According to theory the choice of risk influences the choice of effort. The higher the chosen risk the lower the effort the agents will choose. As Hvide (2002) and Kräkel and Sliwka (2004) show, both agents will choose the same amount of effort in a symmetric tournament in the second stage. Hence, the winning probability is $\frac{1}{2}$ no matter which risk has been chosen. Therefore, both agents will prefer the high risk at the first stage as it does not alter their chance of winning but reduces effort costs. As this prediction is not obvious (compare Lazear and Rosen (1981) footnote 1 or Hvide (2002) page 884) it is interesting to study risk-taking behavior empirically.

The results from our controlled laboratory experiment show that the players act in line with theory in the effort stage and adjust their behavior to the risk chosen in the first stage. However, regarding the risk stage our results do not support theory as only 50% of the players prefer the high risk. Furthermore, a deeper analysis shows that the players only take their own risk choice into account and not that of their opponents when deciding about effort. This also contradicts the theoretical prediction. Yet, the stated beliefs of the players about the effort choice of their opponent's enable us to shed light on their decision process. Our results show that the estimation of the opponents effort is based solely on the risk choice of the opponent and not on overall risk. Hence, the players expect their opponents' to use a similar decision process as they use themselves by only taking the own risk choice into account.

The remainder of the chapter is organized as follows. In Section 3.2 we introduce the model and analyze the subgame-perfect equilibria. Section 3.3 describes the experimental design and procedures. The hypotheses are introduced in Section 3.4 and in Section 3.5 we present the experimental results which are discussed in Section 3.6. Section 3.7 concludes.

3.2 Theoretical Analysis

The experimental set-up is based on the research of Hvide (2002) and Kräkel and Sliwka (2004)[2]. Following their analysis we present a tournament model with the choice of risk as an endogenous variable. In contrast to Kräkel and Sliwka (2004) we concentrate on the special case without differences in the ability of the agents to keep our model as simple as possible. For the same reason we do not consider a random shock that consists of two components, a background noise and an endogenous chosen noise, like Hvide (2002).[3]

3.2.1 The Model

We consider a simple two-stage tournament between two risk-neutral agents A and B. The production function of an agent i $(i = A, B)$ will be described

---

[2]Note that we do not analyze a principal agent model where the principal optimally designs the tournament game but concentrate on the behavior of the agents.

[3]Of course in the real world tournaments are used if there are high common shocks or if only ordinal information is available at reasonable costs. We could integrate a common shock into our design which would not alter the results as common shocks cancel each other out in a tournament.

by

$$y_i = e_i + \varepsilon_i$$

where e_i denotes the effort level of the agent i which cannot be observed by others. The individual noise term which we will also refer to as random shock is specified by ε_i. ε_A and ε_B are assumed to be stochastically independent and normally distributed with $\varepsilon_i \sim N\left(0, \sigma_{r_i}^2\right)$. The agents' cost functions are assumed to be symmetric with $c(e_i)$ and $c'(e_i) > 0$, $c''(e_i) > 0$. We assume that the y_i are uncontractable. However, the ordinal ranking of the performance results is verifiable. Hence, the optimal contract can only specify a wage payment conditional on this ranking information. The optimal contract is, therefore, a tournament.

The model starts with the first stage (risk stage), where both agents simultaneously choose the risk of their strategy, r_i, with

$$r_i \in \{L, H\} \text{ and } \sigma_H^2 > \sigma_L^2.$$

The agents have the chance to increase the variance of the noise term and thereby to induce a mean-preserving spread of y_i.

Each agent observes the chosen risk in the second stage (effort stage) and decides on his effort e_i. Both agents compete for the given prizes of the tournament w_1 and w_2 with $w_1 > w_2 \geq 0$. Hence, w_1 is the winner and w_2 is the loser prize. Δw denotes the prize spread $w_1 - w_2$. The agent i will win the tournament and receive w_1 if $y_i > y_j$ whereas agent j gets the loser prize w_2 $(i, j = A, B; i \neq j)$.

3.2.2 Equilibrium Analysis

We now analyze the subgame-perfect equilibria of the considered two-stage game. Therefore, we start with the second stage and analyze the effort. At this stage the risk choice has already been made and is taken as given. Hence, this stage is similar to a standard tournament model with exogenous random shocks as first proposed by Lazear and Rosen (1981). The expected utility

48

for agent i, U_i, equals

$$U_i = \Pr\{y_i > y_j\} w_1 + (1 - \Pr\{y_i > y_j\}) w_2 - c(e_i)$$

$$\Leftrightarrow \qquad U_i = w_2 + \Delta w \cdot \Pr\{y_i > y_j\} - c(e_i). \qquad (3.1)$$

We denote $G = (\cdot; r_i, r_j)$ as the cumulative distribution function of the composed random variable $\varepsilon_j - \varepsilon_i$. This variable is normally distributed with $\varepsilon_j - \varepsilon_i \sim N\left(0, \sigma_{r_i}^2 + \sigma_{r_j}^2\right)$. Therefore, the probability of winning the tournament is

$$\Pr\{y_i > y_j\} = G\left(e_i - e_j; r_i, r_j\right)$$

As Lazear and Rosen (1981) already discussed, the existence of pure-strategy equilibria is typically not assured automatically in tournament models. Anyhow, if we assume that the following condition holds, we can guarantee the existence of a pure-strategy equilibrium.[4]

$$\frac{\Delta w}{\sqrt{8\pi\sigma_L^2}} \exp\left(-\frac{1}{2}\right) < \min_{e_i} c''(e_i) \qquad (3.2)$$

Proposition 1 *For given risk choices the agents will both exert the following effort*

$$e^*(r_i, r_j) = c'^{-1}\left(\frac{\Delta w}{\sqrt{2\pi\left(\sigma_{r_i}^2 + \sigma_{r_j}^2\right)}}\right). \qquad (3.3)$$

The effort is strictly increasing in Δw and decreasing in $\sigma_{r_i}^2 + \sigma_{r_j}^2$.

Proof: See Appendix.

As both agents exert the same amount of effort, the probability of winning the tournament is $\frac{1}{2}$ and purely random. If the spread between the winner and loser prize Δw increases, winning the tournament is more profitable. Therefore, the agents will exert more effort if the spread rises. The effort will

---

[4]The condition guarantees the concavity of the objective functions. For more details please refer to Kräkel and Sliwka (2004) page 106.

decrease if the tournament becomes more noisy. A higher overall variance of the random shock will reduce the marginal gain of increasing effort.

We go on to analyze the optimal choice of risk of each agent in stage 1. We already know that a higher overall variance will induce a reduction of the equilibrium effort. Notice that the choice of risk will not affect the winning probability because, as already mentioned above, both agents will exert the same effort for a given level of risk.

Proposition 2 *The agents will always choose the risky strategy r_H with the higher variance σ_H^2. The choice of risk is therefore $(r_i, r_j) = (H, H)$.*

Proof: See Appendix.

Both agents want to increase the risk by choosing the random shock with high variance. This choice induces a mean-preserving spread of y_i which has no direct effect on the expected output. Choosing a higher risk in practice means choosing riskier projects. The intuition for Proposition 2 is that the agents have an incentive to raise the noise of the tournament and thereby reduce the effort level they will choose in the second stage.[5] Hence, by choosing the high risk strategy the agents can commit themselves to exerting less effort which reduces their costs but does not alter their winning probabilities.

3.3 Experimental Design and Procedure

We implemented the simple rank-order tournament with endogenous risk choice in a controlled laboratory experiment. As we assume in the theoretical model that only ordinal ranking information is verifiable, the players were paid based on their ordinal ranking as well. The experiment consisted of 27 rounds and 30 participants and we collected 810 observations. In each of the 27 rounds two players were matched together randomly and anonymously. Hence, each participant played 27 times and each time with a different opponent. We implemented a perfect stranger matching to prevent reputation

---

[5]Note that this result can be generalized for risk-averse agents as well. For further details please compare Hvide (2002) page 885.

effects or reciprocity. The theoretical predictions for the experimental game are independent of finite repetition as the repeated game involves the choice of the Nash Equilibrium's risk and effort levels of the one-shot game in each round. In this experiment the players had to choose between two different distributions of random shock which only differed in variance. After they had both chosen the distribution of risk simultaneously and observed the choice of their opponent, they chose effort.

The experiment was conducted at the Cologne Laboratory of Economic Research at the University of Cologne in June 2007. Altogether 30 students participated in the experiment. They were all enrolled in the Faculty of Management, Economics, and Social Sciences and had completed their second year of studies. For the recruitment of the participants we used the online recruitment system by Greiner (2003). We used the experimental software z-tree by Fischbacher (2007) for programming the experiment.

At the outset of the session the subjects were randomly assigned to a cubicle where they took a seat in front of a computer terminal. The instructions were handed out and read out by the experimenters.[6] After that the subjects had time to ask questions if they had any difficulties in understanding the instructions. Communication - other than with the experimental software - was not allowed.

The session started with six trial rounds so that the players could get used to the game. In the trial rounds each player had the opportunity to simulate the game by choosing the strategies for both players and observing the outcomes. These trial rounds were not related to any payment. Then the 27 main rounds started. All rounds were identical but played with a different partner. In each round the player with the higher final score won the tournament. The final score was the sum of the points the player could choose (effort) and additional points that were drawn from a normal distribution (random shock).

At the beginning of each round the players had to choose between two states A and B. If they chose state A (low variance) the additional points were drawn from a normal distribution with a mean of zero points and a

---

[6]The full set of all instructions translated into English can be found in the Appendix.

standard deviation of 23.1 points. If they chose state B (high variance) the additional points were drawn from a normal distribution with a mean of zero points and a standard deviation of 46.2 points. After they had chosen the state they were informed about the decision their opponent made. Hence, the information about the states was common knowledge. Then both players were asked to choose a number of points between zero and 100 (inclusive) simultaneously. The higher the number of points chosen, the higher were the costs of that decision for the player. Each player was given a cost table where the costs were calculated using the cost function $c(e_i) = \frac{e_i^2}{100}$. Additionally the players were also asked to report their belief about the number of points their opponent would choose. After they had chosen their number and reported their belief they observed their additional points and the final scores of both players. They were also informed which player was the winner of the round. This information enabled the players to learn over the course of the experiment. At the end of the 27 rounds one of the rounds was drawn by lot. Each player who won the tournament in which he participated in the drawn round earned the winner prize of 159 taler, each loser earned the loser prize of 100 taler. The costs for the number of points chosen were subtracted from the prize. All players who had reported a correct belief received a bonus of 15 taler if the belief was exactly the number of points chosen by their opponent. If the belief was within one point of the amount chosen the player received twelve talers if it differed two points he received nine talers and so on. If the belief deviated more than four points no reward was paid. Additionally all subjects received a show up fee of 2.50 Euro independent of their status as winner or loser. The exchange rate was 0.16 Euro per taler and on average the players earned 19.81 Euro in this experiment. After the last round the subjects were requested to complete a questionnaire including questions on gender and age. Furthermore, this questionnaire contained questions concerning the subject's risk attitude. As in the previous chapter these questions were taken from the German Socio Economic Panel and dealt with the overall risk attitude of the subject. The whole procedure took about one and a half hour.

3.4 Hypotheses

First of all, based on the theoretical reasoning above, we start by investigating the choice of effort. At this stage of the game the decision about risk has already been made. Therefore, it should be taken as exogenous in this stage. Nevertheless, the players should react to the difference of the variance of the random shock and exert more effort if the overall variance is lower. The lowest effort should be exerted (in this experiment symbolized as the choice of the number of points) if both players have chosen state B (high variance) which we will denote as state 1. In contrast we expect the effort chosen by the players to be highest if both have chosen the state A (we call that state 3 or low variance). If one player has chosen state A and the other state B (referred to as state 2) the effort chosen should be higher than in state 1 and lower than in state 3 (Hypothesis 1).

Of course, the model makes a more precise prediction if we -like in the theoretical model- assume that the agents are risk-neutral.[7] If the players are in state 1 they should choose 18 points in equilibrium (Hypothesis 1.1). In state 3 they should choose 36 points in equilibrium (Hypothesis 1.2). The number of points chosen in state 2 should be 23 in equilibrium (Hypothesis 1.3). We do not expect the participants of the experiment to understand the game perfectly. But they should at least come closer to the equilibrium over the course of the experiment.

Let us now take a look at the hypothesis regarding the choice of risk. We expect the players to choose state B with the high variance in all cases. Although we cannot expect that participants in the experiment are able to understand the game perfectly, the data should at least show that the players learn state B is the best choice over time (Hypothesis 2).

According to theory only the overall variance matters. Therefore, there should be no difference in the strategy of the player if he has chosen state A and his opponent state B or if the situation is reversed. The effort exerted in both cases should be equal (Hypothesis 3).

---

[7]The effort of risk-averse players should be lower in equilibrium. Compare Kräkel (forthcoming).

3.5 Results

We start by investigating the effort (number of points) chosen by the players after they have observed which state of risk their opponent has selected. Figure 3.1 shows the mean and the standard deviation of effort sorted by state. 188 (23.21%) of our 810 observations are of state 1 (high/high) and we have 202 (24.94%) of our observations in state 3 (low/low).

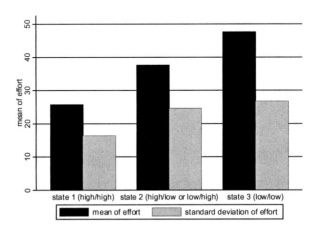

Figure 3.1: Mean of effort and standard deviation sorted by state

As the likelihood of being in state 2 is twice as large as being in state 1 respectively 3 we have 420 (51.85%) observations in state 2. In state 1 where both players have selected the high variance the effort chosen is the lowest with a mean of 25.73 compared to the other states. With a mean of 47.55 the players choose the highest effort in state 3 with the low variance for both players. The effort chosen in state 2 is higher than in state 1 and lower than in state 2. On average the players exert an effort of 37.57 in state 2. These observations are well in line with the theoretical prediction that the effort rises if the overall variance declines. Note that the standard deviation of the effort chosen also varies with the state the players are facing. The higher the mean of effort the higher is the standard deviation. To test whether the state has an effect on the choice of effort we run regressions. In all cases the dependent variable is the effort. The results are reported in Table 3.1.

	(1)[+] OLS	(2)[+] OLS	(3) Fixed	(4) Fixed
State 1	−11.840***	−11.780***	−3.180***	−3.142***
	(3.95)	(3.93)	(1.15)	(1.13)
State 3	9.981***	10.140***	2.588**	2.767**
	(2.93)	(2.88)	(1.13)	(1.11)
Round		−0.284**		−0.273***
		(0.12)		(0.05)
Constant	37.570***	41.500***	37.410***	41.180***
	(4.11)	(4.80)	(0.60)	(0.95)
Observations	810	810	810	810
adj. R^2	0.0920	0.0989	0.0194[++]	0.0505[++]

[+]Robust standard errors in parentheses are calculated by clustering on subjects
[++]We report the within R^2 for the fixed effects regressions
***$p < 0.01$, **$p < 0.05$, *$p < 0.10$

Table 3.1: Regressions for effort dependent on state

We use dummy variables for the states 1 and 3 as independent variables in all regressions. The dummy variable for state 1 (3) is one if the players are in state 1 (3) and zero otherwise. State 2, therefore, is the reference category in these regressions. We control for time trends by using the variable round which counts the rounds of the experiment.[8] As one subject plays the game 27 times we compute robust standard errors adjusted for intraperson correlation. The first regression (1) is a simple OLS. Regarding the results of this regression we show that both dummies for the states are highly significant.

---

[8]We also do regressions including period^2 to control for non-linear time trends but the results do not change. The variable period^2 does not show any significant influence.

As the reference category is state 2 the regression predicts that players choose an average effort of 37.57 if they are in state 2. The effort declines about 11.84 if the players are in state 1 with the high overall variance. Furthermore, the regression shows that the effort selected by the players rises about 9.981 compared to state 2 if they are in state 3. The results do not change qualitatively if we control for variables like gender or the risk attitude of the players.[9] We also run fixed effects regressions reported in columns (3) and (4) of Table 3.1 which show qualitatively the same results.[10] The players act well in line with theory and adjust to the different variances of the random shock. If the tournament contains more noise in terms of a higher overall variance the players reduce their effort significantly and choose a lower number of points.

	Effort Theoretical mean	Effort Empirical mean	Effort Standard error	p-value
State 1	18	25.73	1.18	0.0000
State 2	23	37.57	1.20	0.0000
State 3	36	47.55	1.88	0.0000

Table 3.2: One sample mean comparison test

Yet, we have also seen that the mean of effort chosen is always higher than predicted by the theoretical equilibrium. Note that most of the players (more than 60%) state risk neutrality in our questionnaire so that we can expect them to choose the effort level predicted for risk-neutral players.[11] To check whether the difference is significant we do a one sample mean comparison test for each state and compare the theoretical and empirical mean of effort.

---

[9]Please refer to Table 3.6 in the Appendix for the complete results.

[10]Additionally we analyzed the results of only the first period as this is similar to a one shot game. The jonckheere-trepstra test shows that there are significant differences in the effort choice depending on state. Thus the behavior in the first period is in line with the behavior in the pooled data.

[11]Compare Figure 3.5 and Table 3.7 in the Appendix for an overview of the risk attitudes of the players. We do not find any significant differences in effort levels when comparing risk-neutral players to the others.

The results are reported in Table 3.2. In all states the empirical mean is significantly higher than the theoretical mean. This behavior has occurred in many experiments, compare for example Bull et al. (1987) or Wu and Roe (2005). Grund and Sliwka (2005) offer a possible explanation and show that inequity-averse agents exert higher effort levels than purely self-interested ones.

A look at regression (2) in Table 3.1 shows that the variable round has a significant negative influence on the effort exerted. Hence, the players learn over the course of the experiment and get closer to the equilibrium.[12]

We can summarize the observations as follows.

Result 1 (Hypothesis 1): *If the players are in state 1 (high/high) their effort chosen is significantly lower than in state 2 (high/low or low/high). The effort is highest if they are in state 3 (low/low). Hence, the players act in line with Hypothesis 1 and adjust their behavior according to the overall variance. However, we have to reject Hypothesis 1.1, 1.2 and 1.3 because the players choose a significantly higher effort level in all states as compared to the equilibrium predictions. We observe learning behavior which directs the players closer to equilibrium over the course of the experiment.*

Now we investigate the choice of risk. As we pointed out in Hypothesis 2 the players should prefer state B with the high variance in equilibrium. 49.14% of the players choose state B (high variance) and 50.86% of the players prefer state A (low variance) instead. Hence, the players do not act in line with theory. Looking at Figure 3.2 we see that this behavior does not change over the course of the experiment. The players do not learn that state B should be favored. One possible reason for this observation might be the fact that a certain amount of players (13) stick to their decision over all 27 rounds. Seven of the players always choose state A and six always prefer state B. We have to reject Hypothesis 2.

---

[12] Check Figure 3.6 in the Appendix for a graphical overview.

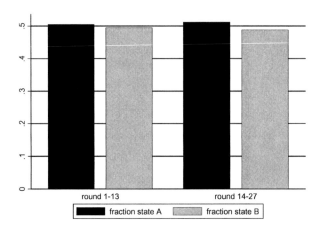

Figure 3.2: Fraction of the choice of state for two sub-periods

Result 2 (Hypothesis 2): *The players choose state A in 50.86% of the cases and state B in 49.14% of the cases. The players do not change their behavior over the course of the experiment. Hence, Hypothesis 2 has to be rejected.*

To investigate Hypothesis 3 we have to divide state 2 into two different states 2a an 2b. In state 2a the player has chosen the high variance and his opponent the low one. The opposite is true for state 2b. In this state the player has picked the low variance and his opponent the high one. Figure 3.3 shows the mean and the standard deviation of effort sorted by the divided states. We see that the players act differently in state 2a (high/low) and 2b (low/high). In state 2a the mean effort is 26.85 and in state 2b the mean is 48.30. To test whether the means of state 2a and 2b are significantly different we execute a Wilcoxon matched-pairs signed rank test. The mean of effort chosen in state 2a is significantly different from the mean of effort chosen in state 2b.[13] Therefore, we cannot treat state 2a and state 2b as the same state as theory predicts. A look at Figure 3.3 shows that the players do

---

[13]See Table 3.8 in the Appendix for details of the test.

not seem to consider the risk choice of their opponent when selecting their effort. On average the players choose a higher effort if they have selected state A (low variance) than if they have selected state B (high variance). The means of state 1 and state 2a are very similar and the same is true for the means of state 2b and 3. In contrast to that the means of state 2a and 2b are significantly different. The standard deviations of effort follow the same pattern.

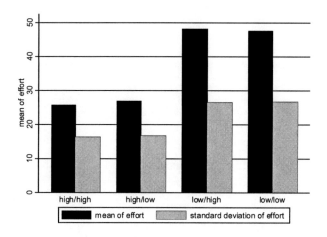

Figure 3.3: Mean of effort and standard deviation sorted by state with state 2 divided in state 2a and state 2b

These observations suggest that players only react to the variance of the random shock that they have chosen and do not take into account the choice of their opponents. Then the choice of state A or B should be sufficient to explain the choice of effort. We investigate this by using regressions. The dependent variable is the effort chosen by the player and we compute robust standard errors by clustering on subjects. The independent variables are dummy variables. The first one is a dummy for the choice of state the player himself has made whereas the second one is a dummy variable for the choice of state of his opponent. Both are one if state B is chosen and zero otherwise.

	(1)+	(2)+	(3)	(4)
	OLS	OLS	Fixed	Fixed
Dummy state player	−21.61***	−21.62***	−10.64***	−10.64***
	(6.15)	(6.14)	(1.40)	(1.40)
Dummy state opponent		−0.17		−0.05
		(0.98)		(0.84)
Constant	47.93***	48.02***	42.54***	42.57***
	(5.53)	(5.42)	(0.80)	(0.90)
Observations	810	810	810	810
adj. R^2	0.1909	0.1899	0.0691++	0.0691++

+Robust standard errors in parentheses are calculated by clustering on subjects

++We report the within R^2 for the fixed effects regressions

***$p < 0.01$, **$p < 0.05$, *$p < 0.10$

Table 3.3: Regressions for effort dependent on choice of risk of the players

The results are reported in Table 3.3. In regression (1) we see that the players choose an average effort of 47.93 if they have selected state A (low variance). The effort chosen declines significantly if they have selected the high variance (state B). The effort is 21.61 points lower on average if the players are in state B compared to state A. Regression (2) contains a dummy for the choice of state of the opponent, too. If the players take the choice of risk of their opponent into account this variable should have a significant influence on the effort chosen by the player. We see that the dummy shows no significant influence and the coefficient is very small. This result does not change if we insert other control variables like gender or risk attitude and we observe learning behavior if we include the variable round.[14] The fixed effects regressions reported in columns (3) and (4) also lead to qualitatively similar results. Looking at the adjusted R^2 we observe that it is higher if we use the individual risk choice as an independent variable than if we use the state

---

[14]Compare Table 3.9 in the Appendix for details of the regressions.

which denotes the overall risk like in Table 3.1. Hence, we can conclude that the players focus on their own decision about the risk in a tournament. The risk choice of their opponent is only of minor importance for their decision on the effort.

Result 3 (Hypothesis 3): *The players choose a significantly lower effort if they are in state 2a (high/low) than in state 2b (low/high). The experimental results show that the players do not act in line with the prediction that they should take into account the overall variance and not only the one they have selected. Therefore, we have to reject Hypothesis 3.*

In our experiment we have also collected information about the players' belief about the effort of their opponent. This enables us to investigate (*i*) the players ability to estimate the effort of their opponent correctly and what drives this estimation and (*ii*) if the players act rationally and exert the optimal effort for their given belief. We see in Table 3.4 that the overall mean of the difference between belief of the player and the true effort of his opponent is close to zero.

	Mean	Standard deviation
State 1 (high/high)	6.70	22.66
State 2 (high/low or low/high)	0.15	33.66
State 3 (low/low)	− 3.32	36.98
State 2a (high/low)	−11.82	32.51
State 2b (low/high)	12.32	30.44
Overall	0.81	32.52

Table 3.4: Mean and standard deviation difference between player's belief and partner's effort

Compare Figure 3.4 for a graphical overview. If we split our observations according to state we see that the mean is highest in state 1 where both players have chosen the high variance and close to zero in state 2. In state 1 the player overestimates and in state 3 the player underestimates the effort of his opponent. As we have already mentioned the players react differently in state $2a$ and $2b$ and therefore we have to split state 2. The difference between the belief of the player and the true effort of his opponent is higher in state $2a$ and $2b$ than in state 1 or 3.

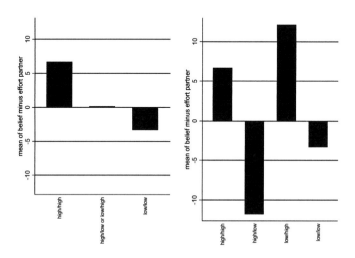

Figure 3.4: Mean of difference between belief of the player and effort of partner by state

If the player has chosen a high variance and his opponent a low one the player underestimates the effort of his opponent. The opposite is true if he has chosen a low variance and his opponent a high one. In this case he overestimates the effort of his opponent. Thus the player overestimates the true effort of his opponent if the opponent has chosen a high risk and underestimates effort if his opponent has chosen a low risk. If both players have chosen the same amount of risk the difference between the belief and the true effort is lower than if the players have chosen different amounts of risk. It is quite intuitive that it is more difficult to put oneself into the position of the opponent if he has chosen a different amount of risk. The highest average deviation is 12.32 in state 2b. On average the players have a good feeling for the effort their opponent will expend. To investigate what determines the beliefs of the players we run regressions with the belief as the dependent variable. The results show that the players formulate their beliefs based upon the choice of risk of their opponent but do not take into account their own risk choice.[15] As we have seen the selected risk influences the choice of effort of the players and the selected risk of the opponent influences the stated belief. Hence, the players assume that their opponents act the same way they act themselves.

	Mean	Mean 1-13	Mean 14-27
State 1 (high/high)	8.78	11.44	6.34
State 2 (high/low or low/high)	17.86	19.06	16.71
State 3 (low/low)	21.05	26.03	16.72
State 2a (high/low)	6.46	7.88	5.09
State 2b (low/high)	29.26	30.24	28.31
Overall	16.55	18.98	14.29

Table 3.5: Mean of difference between effort and theoretical effort by state and subperiod

The next issue we investigate is whether the players act rationally and exert the optimal effort given their stated belief. We can derive the optimal effort for each belief the player has about the true effort of his opponent. Of course the optimal reaction depends not only on the belief of the player but also on the state. Therefore, we have three reaction functions, one for each state.[16] The difference between the effort the player really exerts and the best response effort shows how much the player deviates from optimal behavior if he acts according to his belief. Table 3.5 shows the mean of that difference sorted by state. As we have already mentioned the players exert

---

[15] Compare Table 3.10 in the Appendix.

[16] Compare Figure 3.7 in the Appendix.

more effort than the theory would predict in all states. Again the players act differently in state 2a and 2b. The highest deviation of the optimal effort occurs in the state 2b and 3. In both states the player has selected the low risk and selects an effort that is too high compared to the optimal one. But as can be seen from a comparison of the last two columns in Table 3.5 we observe learning behavior over the course of the experiment. The effort of the players differs less from the optimal one in the second half of the experiment. By investigating the belief of the players we gain insight into their strategies. The average difference between the belief and the true effort of the opponent is relatively small. Hence, the players have a good intuition about the behavior of their opponent. By comparing the difference between the optimal effort and the exerted effort for a given belief we are able to investigate the rationality of the players behavior. Over the course of the experiment the players develop a better understanding and get closer to the optimal effort for a stated belief. This explains the learning behavior which we observe in Hypothesis 1.

3.6   Discussion

The experimental results of Section 3.5 have revealed two interesting observations which contradict the theoretical predictions. (1) the players do not take into account the overall risk when deciding about effort and (2) they do not always prefer high risk in the first stage. First we will provide possible explanations for these findings and then discuss the implications of our results in general.

The results show that the players only respond to their own risk choice when they decide about effort. It is interesting to investigate why the players fail to act in line with theory and what drives their decisions. We are able to shed some light on the decision process of the players by using their stated beliefs. The analysis has shown that players state their beliefs about the effort of their opponent based solely on the risk decision of the opponent. Hence, the players understand that the opponent's risk influences the opponent's decision at the effort stage. In other words, they expect their opponents to take into account the same decision variable (only own risk choice) as they do themselves. This suggests that the players do not act completely rational as the theory assumes. In a first step they act rational because they know if they choose high risk they should prefer low effort. Hence, they understand the impact of their own risk choice on their own effort level. In a second step however, the players fail to understand that they should take into account the overall risk and therefore also the risk choice of their opponent when deciding about their effort. They do not enter this level of reasoning which requires comprehending that in a tournament the overall risk matters because it is a relative performance evaluation. The so called depth-of-reasoning have for example been studied by Nagel (1995), Ho et al. (1998) or Camerer (2003).

At the risk-taking stage only about half of the players choose the high risk which is not in line with theory. It might not seem unreasonable to suppose that the risk attitude of the players could help to solve this puzzle. But already Hvide (2002) states there is no difference in the optimal risk choice of risk-neutral and risk-averse agents.[17] Indeed, we do not find significant influence of the risk attitude on the risk choice in our data either (see Table 3.11 in the Appendix). As we already mentioned in Section 3.5 most of the players state a quite risk-neutral attitude in our questionnaire. Hence, the risk attitude of the players does not explain this puzzle. We also check whether age, gender or round have an impact on the choice of risk but do not find any significant influences (see also Table 3.11 in the Appendix).

Yet, recall that choosing the high risk does no longer serve as a commitment device to reduce effort of both players at the second stage if the risk choice has no impact on the effort decision of the opponent. Nevertheless, following theory, the players should prefer high risk to a least reduce their own effort and effort costs. However, a reason for preferring low risk might be that the players think they can gain more control over the outcome of the game if they choose low risk.

---

[17]With homogeneous agents there is a symmetric equilibrium at the effort stage and the winning probability is therefore $\frac{1}{2}$ no matter which risk the agents prefer. Hence, the choice of risk only influences the amount of effort chosen and not the income risk. It is therefore the best option for two risk-averse agents to choose the high risk as well and thereby reduce the costs of effort.

To solve the risk stage of the tournament one needs to find a subgame-perfect equilibrium. There are several papers discussing the fact that in experiments or the real world subgame-perfect equilibria or even Nash Equilibria are not played. Compare for example the seminal article of Selten (1978) or the papers of Johnson et al. (2002) or Binmore et al. (2002) which show that players do not tend to use backward induction in bargaining games. Perhaps the most likely explanation for this kind of risk-taking behavior in our experiment is that it is cognitively too demanding for the participants to use backward induction. As we have seen the players are already overstrained to solve the Nash Equilibrium at the second stage correctly by taking into account the overall variance. Hence, it is very likely that they also fail to solve the more complex subgame-perfect Nash Equilibrium at the first stage.[18]

In this chapter we concentrate on the behavior of the agents and not on the design of an optimal contract from the principal's point of view. We do this for simplicity and because many situations in the real world have the structure of tournaments but there is no principal who designs an optimal contract as for instance in litigation contests, R&D races or political elections. Nevertheless, it is interesting to mention the implications our research may have for contract design. From the principal's point of view the purpose of a tournament is to induce incentives to work. If risk is a choice variable in a tournament and the risk is not limited the agents will choose infinite risk and zero effort. However, in the real world in situations such as sports contests or promotion tournaments the agents will not be able to choose unlimited risk. Hence, following theory the agents would prefer the highest risk possible and low effort. Nevertheless, given unlimited liability and risk-neutral agents the principal would be able to induce first best effort by changing the spread between winner and loser prizes. As Hvide (2002) argues the fear of excessive risk-taking might be an explanation for why CEOs are not paid solely based

---

[18]Goeree and Holt (2001) and Selten and Stoecker (1986) argue that learning from past experience affects behavior in experiments. However, in our experiment the players have many opportunities to learn. In the trial rounds they could simulate the strategies for both players and observe the outcomes. Anyhow, the risk-taking behavior does not change significantly over the course of the experiment which would be an indicator of learning effects.

on their ordinal ranking (compare for example Murphy (1999) or Garvey and Milbourn (2003)). Yet, we observe tournaments in the real world because they are needed if only ordinal ranking information is observable. Moreover, in a tournament the principal can ex ante commit herself to pay a certain amount of money to the best performing employees. Hence, in contrast to other payment schemes like for example piece rates, tournaments also reduce the danger of opportunistic behavior of the principal (compare Malcomson (1984) and Malcomson (1986)). If we look at our findings we see that the players in the laboratory indeed reduce their effort if they have chosen high risk. On the other hand only 50% of them prefer the high risk option and not 100% of them as the theory suggested. Of course, we have to be very careful when transferring our findings from the laboratory to the real working environment. Nevertheless, if the agents in the real world act similar as the players in the experiment we should not have to worry as much about excessive risk-taking in the real world.

3.7 Conclusion

We investigate a rank-order tournament with two stages in a controlled laboratory experiment. At the first stage the agents decide about risk. After they have observed the overall risk they choose their effort in the second stage. We test whether the players act in line with the theoretical predictions of tournament theory. It predicts that all agents should choose the high risk in the first stage. In our experiment the agents prefer the high risk in 49.14% of the cases. Therefore, we are not able to confirm this prediction. Nevertheless, in the second stage the agents respond to the different variances of random shock. They exert less effort if the variance of the random shock is high which is in line with theory. As has already been observed in other experiments with tournaments, the agents exert more effort than the theory predicts. We observe a reduction of effort over the course of the experiment. This learning behavior can be explained by the fact that the players develop a better understanding of what effort is optimal for a given belief and state. There is no difference in theory between cases in which the agent selects the high risk and his opponent the low one and cases in which the agent chooses the low and his opponent the high risk. Our data shows that in the experiment the agents react differently in these cases. They mainly focus on their own decision and adjust their effort not to the overall risk but to their own choice of risk. If they have chosen the high risk, they exert less effort than if they have selected the low risk.

There are many open questions for further research. It would be interesting for example to investigate this topic with a real-effort task or to explore how the contestants act if the risk choice is continuous. As this chapter only deals with homogeneous agents a further step would be to study the behavior of heterogeneous agents as well which we will do in the following chapter.

3.8 Appendix to Chapter 3

Proof of Proposition 1: Given that Condition 3.2 is met, the first order conditions of the agents' utility will characterize the equilibrium. Notice that for all $i = A, B$ the first order condition is

$$\frac{\partial U_i}{\partial e_i} = \Delta w \cdot g\left(e_i - e_j; r_i, r_j\right) - \frac{\partial c_i}{\partial e_i} \overset{!}{=} 0.$$

$$\Leftrightarrow \quad \Delta w \cdot g\left(e_i - e_j; r_i, r_j\right) = \frac{\partial c_i}{\partial e_i}$$

And we know that

$$\frac{\partial \Pr\left\{y_i > y_j\right\}}{\partial e_i} = \frac{\partial G\left(e_i - e_j; r_i, r_j\right)}{\partial e_i} = g\left(e_i - e_j; r_i, r_j\right)$$

$$= \frac{\partial \Pr\left\{y_j > y_i\right\}}{\partial e_j} = \frac{\partial\left[1 - G\left(e_i - e_j; r_i, r_j\right)\right]}{\partial e_j}$$

Therefore, the left hand-sides of the first order condition are identical for both agents. Hence, we have a symmetric equilibrium where both agents exert identical effort with

$$e_i^*(r_i, r_j) = e_j^*(r_i, r_j) = e^*(r_i, r_j) = c'^{-1}\left(\frac{\Delta w}{\sqrt{2\pi\left(\sigma_{r_i}^2 + \sigma_{r_j}^2\right)}}\right).$$

■

Proof of Proposition 2: For a given strategy r_j player i will prefer a high risk (σ_H) to a low risk (σ_L) if

$$\Delta w \cdot G\left(e_i - e_j; H, r_j\right) - c\left(e^*\left(H, r_j\right)\right) \geq \Delta w \cdot G\left(e_i - e_j; L, r_j\right) - c\left(e^*\left(L, r_j\right)\right).$$

$$\Leftrightarrow \quad c\left(e^*\left(L, r_j\right)\right) - c\left(e^*\left(H, r_j\right)\right) \geq \Delta w \cdot \left(G\left(e_i - e_j; L, r_j\right) - G\left(e_i - e_j; H, r_j\right)\right)$$

$$\Leftrightarrow \quad c\left(c'^{-1}\left(\frac{\Delta w}{\sqrt{2\pi\left(\sigma_L^2 + \sigma_{r_j}^2\right)}}\right)\right) - c\left(c'^{-1}\left(\frac{\Delta w}{\sqrt{2\pi\left(\sigma_H^2 + \sigma_{r_j}^2\right)}}\right)\right) \geq 0$$

$$\Leftrightarrow \quad c\left(c'^{-1}\left(\frac{\Delta w}{\sqrt{2\pi\left(\sigma_L^2 + \sigma_{r_j}^2\right)}}\right)\right) \geq c\left(c'^{-1}\left(\frac{\Delta w}{\sqrt{2\pi\left(\sigma_H^2 + \sigma_{r_j}^2\right)}}\right)\right)$$

The cost for the effort if the agent has chosen the low risk is always higher than the cost for the effort if he has chosen high risk. Hence, the inequality is always true.

■

| | (1) | (2) |
	OLS	OLS
State 1	−11.910***	−11.850***
	(3.94)	(3.96)
State 3	10.270***	10.100***
	(2.76)	(2.78)
Round	−0.284**	−0.284**
	(0.12)	(0.12)
Gender	−1.635	−0.336
	(8.05)	(10.50)
Risk attitude		0.848
		(2.85)
Constant	41.990***	37.530**
	(5.39)	(17.00)
Observations	810	810
adj. R^2	0.0987	0.0997

Robust standard errors in parentheses are calculated by clustering on subjects
***$p < 0.01$, **$p < 0.05$, *$p < 0.10$

Table 3.6: Regressions for choice of effort dependent on state

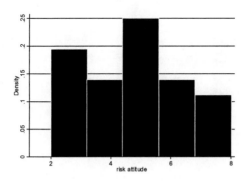

Figure 3.5: Histogram of the risk attitude of the players
(zero is risk-averse and ten is risk loving)

	Percent	cum. Percent
0	0	0
1	0	0
2	3.33	3.33
3	20.00	23.33
4	16.67	40.00
5	30.00	70.00
6	16.67	86.67
7	6.67	93.33
8	6.67	100.00
9	0	100.00
10	0	100.00
Mean	4.83	

Table 3.7: Fraction of the risk attitude of the players

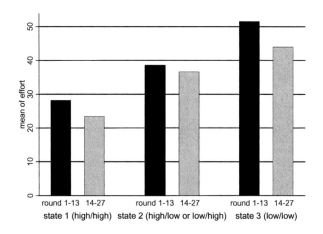

Figure 3.6: Mean of effort sorted by state and subperiods

	Effort Mean	Effort Standard error	p-value
(high/low)	26.85	1.15	0.000
(low/high)	48.30	1.83	

Table 3.8: Wilcoxon matched-pairs signed rank test for condition 2a and 2b

	(1) OLS	(2) OLS	(3) OLS
Dummy state player	−21.670***	−22.330***	−22.250***
	(6.12)	(6.04)	(5.92)
Dummy state opponent	−0.219	−0.193	−0.205
	(1.01)	(1.00)	(0.95)
Round	−0.285**	−0.286**	−0.286**
	(0.12)	(0.12)	(0.12)
Gender		−4.009	−3.637
		(7.54)	(9.58)
Risk attitude			0.236
			(2.52)
Constant	52.070***	53.590***	52.300***
	(5.98)	(6.51)	(15.10)
Observations	810	810	810
adj. R^2	0.1971	0.2015	0.2007

Robust standard errors in parentheses are calculated by clustering on subjects
***$p < 0.01$, **$p < 0.05$, *$p < 0.10$

Table 3.9: Regressions for choice of effort dependent on choice of risk of the players

	(1)	(2)
	OLS[+]	Fixed
Dummy state player	-7.201	-1.335
	(4.63)	(1.62)
Dummy state opponent	-4.715^*	-4.461^{***}
	(2.65)	(0.97)
Round	-0.262^{**}	-0.258^{***}
	(0.10)	(0.06)
Constant	47.650^{***}	44.580^{***}
	(4.96)	(1.37)
Observations	810	810
adj. R^2	0.0440	0.0547^{++}

[+]Robust standard errors in parentheses are calculated by clustering on subjects
[++]We report the within R^2 for the fixed effects regressions
$^{***}p < 0.01$, $^{**}p < 0.05$, $^*p < 0.10$

Table 3.10: Regressions for belief dependent on state

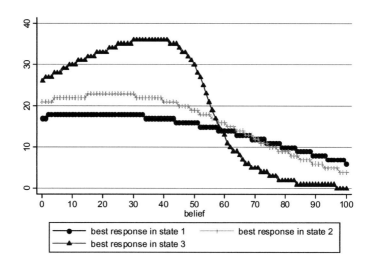

Figure 3.7: Reaction function

| | (1) | (2) |
	Probit	Probit
Risk attitude	−0.0201	−0.1190
	(0.1100)	(0.1400)
Round	−0.0018	−0.0019
	(0.0046)	(0.0049)
Gender		−0.6120
		(0.4900)
Age		0.0949
		(0.0640)
Constant	0.1010	−1.5660
	(0.5600)	(1.8900)
Observations	810	810
Pseudo R^2	0.0005	0.0578
Pseudo Loglikelihood	−561.04073	−528.90240

Robust standard errors in parentheses are calculated by clustering on subjects
***$p < 0.01$, **$p < 0.05$, *$p < 0.10$

Table 3.11: Regressions for choice of risk (zero denotes low risk and one denotes high risk) dependent on the risk attitude of the players

Instructions for the experiment

Welcome to this experiment!

Please read these instructions carefully. If you have any questions please raise your hand and ask us. Please note the following:

- No communication is allowed.

- All decisions are anonymous. None of the other participants will learn the identity of the one who makes a certain decision.

- The payment is anonymous, too. Nobody gets to know how high the payment of another participant is.

Rounds and Partners

- The experiment consists of 27 rounds. At the end of the experiment one of the rounds will be drawn by lot. This round will determine the payment. Please think carefully about your decision as every round will possibly be the round that will be relevant for your payment.

- Before the experiment starts you will have the chance to get a better feeling for it in six trial rounds. These trial rounds have no influence on your payment. Their only purpose is to help you develop a better understanding of the experiment.

- You will play each round with a different partner. The identity of your partner will not be revealed. We have ensured that you will never play with the same partner again.

- If you achieve a higher final score than your partner you will win the game in the round. The final score is the sum of the points you can choose and additional points that are random and depend on the state that you have chosen before.

Progress of one round

- At the beginning of each round you will be matched with one partner.

- At the start of each round you will have to decide between two different states. The variance of the additional points depends on this decision. If you choose state A (low variance) the additional points that will together with your decision determine the final score will be drawn from a normal distribution with a mean of zero and a standard deviation of 23.1 points. If you choose state B (high variance) the additional points will be drawn from a normal distribution with a mean of zero and a standard deviation of 46.2 points. You will find a chart at the end of these instructions to clarify this distribution.

- Your partner can also choose between state A and B.

- After both players have made their decision you will be informed which state your partner has chosen and vice versa. There are 4 possible outcomes in each round:

  - both players choose state A.
  - you choose state A and your partner chooses state B.
  - you choose state B and your partner chooses state A.
  - both players choose state B.

- Please keep in mind that your additional points and the additional points of your partner are completely independent of each other even if you have both chosen the same state.

- Now you will be asked to choose a number between zero and 100 points. The number is more expensive if it is higher. At the end of these instructions you will find a table that shows the costs for each number.

- Your partner is also asked to choose a number between zero and 100 points.

- After you have entered your own number you will be asked to report your belief about the number your partner has chosen. If your belief in this round is correct and this round is relevant for the payment you will receive a reward for your belief. If your belief deviates from the number of points your partner has chosen this reward decreases (for detailed information see below).

- After both players have made their decisions the results of the round will be calculated. Your final score is the sum of the number of points

77

you have chosen and the additional points drawn from the normal distribution. The final score of your partner is calculated in the same way. If your final score is higher than the final score of your partner you are the winner of that round. If your final score is lower you have lost this round. If there is a tie the experimental software will draw the winner by lot.

- After you and your partner have been informed about your final scores and the winner of the round you will be matched with a new partner. The game then starts again.

- You will play 27 rounds with different partners. Please note that you will only play once with a particular partner.

- After the 27 rounds one round is drawn by lot which determines your payment. If you are the winner of that round you will receive the winner prize of 159 taler. The costs for the number you have chosen will be subtracted from this prize. If you have lost this round you will receive the loser prize of 100 taler less the costs for the number you have chosen. Please notice that your final score in that round only determines if you are the winner or the loser of that round. The winner and the loser prize are independent of the final score or the score difference between you and your partner.

- Additionally to the payment of this experiment you receive 2.50 Euro show-up fee which is independent of your status as winner or loser.

- Please fill out the questionnaire which will appear on the screen.

- Please stay at your seat until we call your cubicle number. Please take these instructions and your cubicle number with you. Otherwise we cannot hand out the payment.

- The exchange rate is 0.16 Euro per taler.

Reward for your belief about the number your partner has chosen	
Deviation from the chosen number	
0 points	15 taler
1 point	12 taler
2 points	9 taler
3 points	6 taler
4 points	3 taler
more than 4 points	0 taler

Your payment as winner =
winner prize 159 taler - cost for the chosen number
+ reward + 2.50 Euro show-up fee

Your payment as loser =
loser prize 100 taler - cost for the chosen number
+ reward + 2.50 Euro show-up fee

Thank you for participation and good luck!

Additional comments:

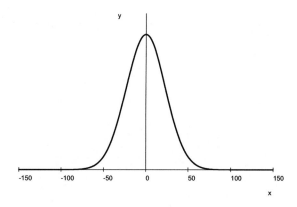

Figure 3.8: State A (low variance): normal distribution
with mean zero and standard deviation 23.1 points

79

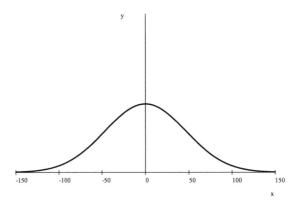

Figure 3.9: State B (high variance): normal distribution
with mean zero and standard deviation 46.2 points

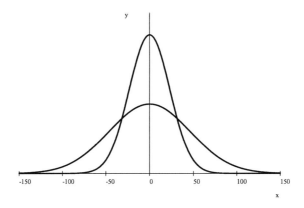

Figure 3.10: Overview of both distributions

Reminder:
The probability that the additional point score belongs to a certain interval
corresponds to the size of the surface under the graph.
If the standard deviation is 23.1 points 95.44% of the drawn points are located
in the interval between -46.2 and 46.2.
If the standard deviation is 46.2 points 95.44% of the drawn points are located
in the interval between -92.4 and 92.4.

Overview of the costs between zero and 100

Please note that the costs are given in taler. Zero points lead to zero costs.

points	1	2	3	4	5	6	7	8	9	10
costs	0.01	0.04	0.09	0.16	0.25	0.36	0.49	0.64	0.81	1

points	11	12	13	14	15	16	17	18	19	20
costs	1.21	1.44	1.69	1.96	2.25	2.56	2.89	3.24	3.61	4

points	21	22	23	24	25	26	27	28	29	30
costs	4.41	4.84	5.29	5.76	6.25	6.76	7.29	7.84	8.41	9

points	31	32	33	34	35	36	37	38	39	40
costs	9.61	10.24	10.89	11.56	12.25	12.96	13.69	14.44	15.21	16

points	41	42	43	44	45	46	47	48	49	50
costs	16.81	17.64	18.49	19.36	20.25	21.16	22.09	23.04	24.01	25

points	51	52	53	54	55	56	57	58	59	60
costs	26.01	27.04	28.09	29.16	30.25	31.36	32.49	33.64	34.81	36

points	61	62	63	64	65	66	67	68	69	70
costs	37.21	38.44	39.69	40.96	42.25	43.56	44.89	46.24	47.61	49

points	71	72	73	74	75	76	77	78	79	80
costs	50.41	51.84	53.29	54.76	56.25	57.76	59.29	60.84	62.41	64

points	81	82	83	84	85	86	87	88	89	90
costs	65.61	67.24	68.89	70.56	72.25	73.96	75.69	77.44	79.21	81

points	91	92	93	94	95	96	97	98	99	100
costs	82.81	84.64	86.49	88.36	90.25	92.16	94.09	96.04	98.01	100

Table 3.12: Cost table

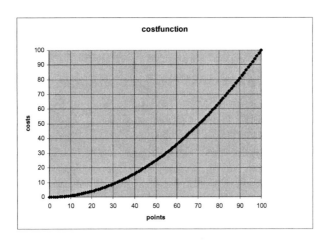

Figure 3.11: Costfunction

Chapter 4

Risk-Taking and Effort in Tournaments with Heterogeneous Agents[1]

4.1 Introduction

This chapter deals with risk and effort choices in winner-take-all competitions or tournaments. In contrast to the previous chapter we focus on heterogeneous agents and investigate unilateral risk-taking. Given a two-player game, either both players are risk takers as in Chapter 3 or a single first mover chooses risk before both players decide on effort/investment. There exist several examples for such unilateral risk-taking. Consider for instance a duopoly where the incumbent firm offers a well-known product and a new firm wants to enter the market. This entrant will first have to decide about the supply of a new kind of product and an innovative marketing strategy. Thereafter, both firms compete for market leadership by choosing their advertising expenditures.

In this chapter, we concentrate on the case of unilateral risk-taking, which has neither theoretically nor experimentally been analyzed so far. The paper of Kräkel (forthcoming) is strongly related to this chapter. He analyzes an

---

[1]This chapter is based upon Kräkel et al. (2008).

asymmetric two-stage tournament with bilateral risk-taking in a continuous setting. Unfortunately, the continuous setting with bilateral risk-taking is so complex that closed-form solutions can hardly be derived. In our model only the challenger chooses risk at the first stage. At the second stage, both the challenger and the incumbent simultaneously decide on efforts or investments. We consider an asymmetric tournament game[2] with discrete choices at the risk and at the effort stage to derive several hypotheses which are then tested in a laboratory experiment. In our asymmetric tournament, a more able player (the "favorite") competes against a less able one (the "underdog").

Consider, for example, the situation with the challenger being the favorite. We can differentiate between three effects that determine his risk-taking: first, as in the previous chapter, risk-taking at stage 1 of the game may influence the equilibrium investments and, hence, investment costs at stage 2 (cost effect). According to this effect, the challenger (as well as the incumbent) prefers a high-risk strategy since high risk reduces overall incentives and, therefore, investment costs at the second stage. Here, as for the homogeneous agents we analyzed in Chapter 3, high risk serves as a commitment device for the players at the second stage, leading to a kind of implicit collusion. Second, the choice of risk by the challenger also influences the players' likelihood of winning. If equilibrium investments do not react to risk-taking the more able challenger will prefer a low-risk strategy to hold his predominant position (likelihood effect). Third, if only the equilibrium investments of the incumbent do react to risk-taking, the more able challenger may choose a high risk to discourage the less able incumbent (discouragement effect). In this situation, high risk destroys the incumbent's incentives at the second stage since it does not pay for him to invest as he would bear high costs but the outcome of the tournament is mainly determined by luck. However, the challenger still invests at the second stage as he has to bear significantly less costs, being the more able player. Such discouragement will be very attractive for the challenger if the gain of winning is rather large.

---

[2]Note that we do not analyze a principal-agent model where the principal optimally designs the tournament game.

The theoretical results show that, in our discrete setting, all three effects will be relevant if the challenger is the favorite whereas taking high risk becomes dominant when the challenger is the underdog. For this reason, our experimental analysis focuses on risk-taking by the favorite and the subsequent investment or effort choices by both players. For each effect we run one treatment with two sessions labeled discouragement treatment, cost treatment, and likelihood treatment. Descriptive results indicate that, contrary to the discouragement effect, both the cost effect and the likelihood effect have impact on the risk choice of the subjects. The results from nonparametric tests and probit regressions reveal that the likelihood effect turns out to be very robust. The two other effects are not confirmed by a Binomial test, but a pairwise comparison of the treatments shows that the findings for the cost effect seem to be more in line with theory than our results for the discouragement effect. Note that in line with the experimental results of Chapter 3 only roughly 55% of the players and not 100% prefer the high risk in the cost treatment. As theoretically predicted, favorites choose significantly more investment or effort than underdogs in the discouragement treatment and the likelihood treatment. In the cost treatment, players' behavior does not significantly differ given low risk, which follows theory, but for high risk underdogs exert clearly more effort than favorites, which contradicts theory. The subjects' effort choices as reactions to given risk are very often in line with theory. Again, the likelihood treatment offers very robust findings. Interestingly, in the two other treatments, favorites tend to react more sensitively to given risk than underdogs although subjects change their roles after each round.

The chapter is organized as follows. The next section introduces the game and the corresponding solution. In Section 4.3, we point out the three main effects of risk-taking – the discouragement effect, the cost effect, and the likelihood effect. In Section 4.4, we describe the experiment. Our testable hypotheses are introduced in Section 4.5. The experimental results are presented in Section 4.6. We discuss three puzzling results in Section 4.7. Section 4.8 concludes.

4.2 The Game

We consider a two-stage tournament game with two risk-neutral players. At the first stage (risk stage), one of the players – the challenger – chooses the variance of the underlying probability distribution that characterizes risk in the tournament. At the second stage (effort stage), both players – the challenger and the incumbent – observe the chosen risk and then simultaneously decide on their efforts.

The player with the better relative performance is declared the winner of the tournament and receives the benefit $B > 0$, whereas the other one gets nothing. Relative performance does not only depend on the effort choices but also on the realization of the underlying noise term.

The two players are heterogeneous in ability. These ability differences are modeled via the players' effort costs. The more able player F ("favorite") has low effort costs, whereas exerting effort entails rather high costs for player U ("underdog"). In particular, both players can only choose between the two effort levels $e_i = e_L$ and $e_i = e_H > 0$ $(i = F, U)$ with $e_H > e_L$ and $\Delta e := e_H - e_L > 0$. The choice of $e_i = e_L$ leads to zero effort costs for player i, but choosing high effort $e_i = e_H$ involves positive costs c_i $(i = F, U)$ with $c_U > c_F > 0$. Relative performance of challenger i is described by

$$RP = e_i - e_j + \varepsilon \qquad (4.1)$$

with ε is noise term which follows a symmetric distribution around zero with cumulative distribution function $G(\varepsilon; \sigma^2)$ and variance σ^2.

At the risk stage, the challenger has to decide between two variances or risks. He can either choose a high risk $\sigma^2 = \sigma_H^2$ or a low risk $\sigma^2 = \sigma_L^2$ with $0 < \sigma_L^2 < \sigma_H^2$. Challenger i is declared winner of the tournament if and only if $RP > 0$. Hence, his winning probability is given by

$$\Pr\{RP > 0\} = 1 - G(e_j - e_i; \sigma^2) = G(e_i - e_j; \sigma^2) \qquad (4.2)$$

where the last equality follows from the symmetry of the distribution. In analogy, we obtain for incumbent j's winning probability:

$$\Pr\{RP < 0\} = G\left(e_j - e_i; \sigma^2\right) = 1 - G\left(e_i - e_j; \sigma^2\right). \tag{4.3}$$

The symmetry of the distribution has two implications: first, each player's winning probability will be $G\left(0; \sigma^2\right) = \frac{1}{2}$ if both choose the same effort level. Second, if both players choose different effort levels, the one with the higher effort has winning probability $G\left(\Delta e; \sigma^2\right) > \frac{1}{2}$, but the player choosing low effort only wins with probability $G\left(-\Delta e; \sigma^2\right) = 1 - G\left(\Delta e; \sigma^2\right) < \frac{1}{2}$. Let

$$\Delta G\left(\sigma^2\right) := G\left(\Delta e; \sigma^2\right) - \frac{1}{2} \tag{4.4}$$

denote the *additional winning probability* of the player with the higher effort level *compared to a situation with identical effort choices* by both players. Note that $\Delta G\left(\sigma^2\right) \in \left(0, \frac{1}{2}\right)$. We assume that increasing risk from σ_L^2 to σ_H^2 shifts probability mass from the mean to the tails so that $G\left(\Delta e; \sigma_L^2\right) > G\left(\Delta e; \sigma_H^2\right)$, implying

$$\Delta G\left(\sigma_L^2\right) > \Delta G\left(\sigma_H^2\right). \tag{4.5}$$

When looking for subgame perfect equilibria by backward induction we start by considering the effort stage 2. Here, both players observe $\sigma^2 \in \{\sigma_L^2, \sigma_H^2\}$ and simultaneously choose their efforts according to the following matrix game:

	$e_F = e_H$	$e_F = e_L$
$e_U = e_H$	$\dfrac{B}{2} - c_U$, $\dfrac{B}{2} - c_F$	$B \cdot G\left(\Delta e; \sigma^2\right) - c_U$, $B \cdot G\left(-\Delta e; \sigma^2\right)$
$e_U = e_L$	$B \cdot G\left(-\Delta e; \sigma^2\right)$, $B \cdot G\left(\Delta e; \sigma^2\right) - c_F$	$\dfrac{B}{2}$, $\dfrac{B}{2}$

The first (second) payoff in each cell refers to player U (F) who chooses rows (columns).

Note that $(e_U, e_F) = (e_H, e_L)$ can never be an equilibrium at the effort stage since

$$B \cdot G\left(-\Delta e; \sigma^2\right) \geq \frac{B}{2} - c_F \Leftrightarrow c_F \geq B \cdot \left(\frac{1}{2} - G\left(-\Delta e; \sigma^2\right)\right)$$

$$\Leftrightarrow \; c_F \geq B \cdot \left(\frac{1}{2} - \left[1 - G\left(\Delta e; \sigma^2\right)\right]\right) \Leftrightarrow c_F \geq B \cdot \Delta G\left(\sigma^2\right)$$

and

$$B \cdot G\left(\Delta e; \sigma^2\right) - c_U \geq \frac{B}{2} \Leftrightarrow B \cdot \Delta G\left(\sigma^2\right) \geq c_U$$

lead to a contradiction as $c_U > c_F$. Combination $(e_U, e_F) = (e_H, e_H)$ will be an equilibrium at the effort stage if and only if

$$\frac{B}{2} - c_i \geq B \cdot G\left(-\Delta e; \sigma^2\right) \Leftrightarrow B \cdot \Delta G\left(\sigma^2\right) \geq c_i$$

holds for player $i = F, U$. In words, each player will not deviate from the high effort level if and only if, compared to $e_i = e_L$, the additional expected gain $B \cdot \Delta G\left(\sigma^2\right)$ is at least as large as the additional costs c_i. Similar considerations for $(e_U, e_F) = (e_L, e_L)$ and $(e_U, e_F) = (e_L, e_H)$ yield the following result:

Proposition 1 *At the effort stage, in equilibrium players U and F choose*

$$(e_U^*, e_F^*) = \begin{cases} (e_H, e_H) & \text{if} \;\; B \cdot \Delta G\left(\sigma^2\right) \geq c_U \\ (e_L, e_H) & \text{if} \;\; c_U \geq B \cdot \Delta G\left(\sigma^2\right) \geq c_F \\ (e_L, e_L) & \text{if} \;\; B \cdot \Delta G\left(\sigma^2\right) \leq c_F \end{cases} \qquad (4.6)$$

Our findings are quite intuitive: the favorite chooses at least as much effort as the underdog because of higher ability and, hence, lower effort costs. If the additional expected gain $B \cdot \Delta G\left(\sigma^2\right)$ is sufficiently large, it will pay off for both players to choose a high effort level. However, for intermediate values of $B \cdot \Delta G\left(\sigma^2\right)$ only the favorite will prefer high effort, and for small values of $B \cdot \Delta G\left(\sigma^2\right)$ neither player exerts high effort.

At the risk stage 1, the challenger chooses risk σ^2. Equations 4.2 and 4.3 show that risk-taking directly influences both players' winning probabilities. Furthermore, Proposition 1 points out that risk also determines the players' effort choices at stage 2. We obtain the following proposition:

Proposition 2 *(i) If $B \leq \frac{c_F}{\Delta G(\sigma_L^2)}$ or $B \geq \frac{c_U}{\Delta G(\sigma_H^2)}$, then the challenger will be indifferent between $\sigma^2 = \sigma_L^2$ and $\sigma^2 = \sigma_H^2$, irrespective of whether he is the favorite or the underdog. (ii) Let $B \in \left(\frac{c_F}{\Delta G(\sigma_L^2)}, \frac{c_U}{\Delta G(\sigma_H^2)} \right)$. When F is the challenger, he will choose $\sigma^2 = \sigma_L^2$ if $B < \frac{c_U}{\Delta G(\sigma_L^2)}$ and $\sigma^2 = \sigma_H^2$ if $B > \frac{c_U}{\Delta G(\sigma_L^2)}$. When U is the challenger, he will always choose $\sigma^2 = \sigma_H^2$.*

Proof: See Appendix.

The result of Proposition 2 (i) shows that risk-taking becomes unimportant if the benefit B is very small or very large. In the first case, it never pays for the players to choose a high effort level, irrespective of the underlying risk. In the latter case, both players prefer to exert high effort for any risk level since winning the tournament is very attractive. Hence, the risk-taking decision is only interesting for moderate benefits that do not correspond to one of these extreme cases.

Proposition 2 (ii) deals with the situation of a moderate benefit. Here, the underdog always prefers the high risk when being the challenger. The intuition for this result comes from the fact that U is in an inferior position at the effort stage according to Proposition 1 (i.e., he will never choose a higher effort than player F), irrespective of the chosen risk level. Therefore, he has nothing to lose and unambiguously gains from choosing the high risk: in case of good luck, he may win the competition despite his inferior position; in case of bad luck, he will not really worsen his position as he has already a rather small winning probability. The favorite is in a completely different situation when being the challenger at the risk stage. According to Proposition 1, he is the presumable winner of the tournament (i.e., he will never choose less effort than player U) and does not want to jeopardize his favorable position. However, Proposition 2 (ii) shows that F's preference for low risk will only hold if the benefit is smaller than a certain cut-off value. If B is rather large, then it will pay for the favorite to choose high risk at stage 1. By this, he strictly gains from discouraging his rival U: given

89

$\sigma^2 = \sigma_L^2$, we have $(e_U^*, e_F^*) = (e_H, e_H)$ at the effort stage, but $\sigma^2 = \sigma_H^2$ induces $(e_U^*, e_F^*) = (e_L, e_H)$.

4.3 Discouragement Effect, Cost Effect and Likelihood Effect

The results of Proposition 2 have shown that the risk behavior of player U is rather uninteresting in this simple discrete setting as he has a (weakly) dominant strategy when being the challenger. Therefore, the remainder of this chapter focuses on the strategic risk-taking of player F. As an illustrating example, consider the case of liberalization of monopoly where a new private entrant can challenge a former public enterprise. In this situation, the former monopolist is typically the weaker player with higher costs whereas the challenger can be roughly characterized as the favorite.[3]

Recall that risk-taking may influence both the players' effort choices and their winning probabilities. As already mentioned in the introduction, in particular three main effects determine the challenger's risk-taking. The first effect is called *discouragement effect*: if F's incentives to win the tournament are sufficiently strong, that is if $B > \max \left\{ \frac{c_F}{\Delta G(\sigma_H^2)}, \frac{c_U}{\Delta G(\sigma_L^2)} \right\}$, he wants to deter U from exerting high effort. From the proof of Proposition 2, we know that low risk σ_L^2 leads to $(e_U^*, e_F^*) = (e_H, e_H)$, but high risk σ_H^2 induces $(e_U^*, e_F^*) = (e_L, e_H)$. Hence, when choosing high risk at stage 1, the favorite completely discourages his opponent and increases his winning probability by $G(\Delta e; \sigma_H^2) - \frac{1}{2} = \Delta G(\sigma_H^2)$, compared to low risk. This effect is shown in Figure 4.1. There, the cumulative distribution function given high risk, $G(\cdot; \sigma_H^2)$, is obtained from the low-risk cdf, $G(\cdot; \sigma_L^2)$, by flattening and clockwise rotation in the point $(0, \frac{1}{2})$. Low risk makes high effort attractive for both players since effort has still a real impact on the outcome of the tour-

---

[3]Such situation is typical for the liberalization of network industries in the European Union, in particular for the telecommunication market and the airline sector; see, among many others, Geradin (2006). For economic modeling of the new entrant as the low-cost firm and the incumbent being the high-cost firm, see, for example, Caplin and Nalebuff (1986).

nament, resulting into a winning probability of $\frac{1}{2}$ for each player. Switching to a high risk strategy σ_H^2 now increases the effort difference $e_F^* - e_U^*$ by Δe, which raises F's likelihood of winning by $\Delta G\left(\sigma_H^2\right)$ without influencing his effort costs.

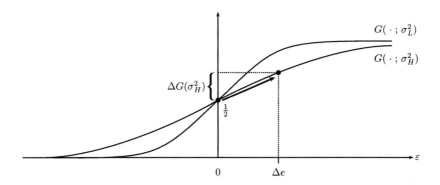

Figure 4.1: Discouragement effect

The second effect can be labeled *cost effect*. In our discrete setting, this effect will determine F's risk choice if $\frac{c_U}{\Delta G\left(\sigma_L^2\right)} < B < \frac{c_F}{\Delta G\left(\sigma_H^2\right)}$.[4] In this situation, $\sigma^2 = \sigma_L^2$ leads to $(e_U^*, e_F^*) = (e_H, e_H)$ at stage 2, but $\sigma^2 = \sigma_H^2$ implies $(e_U^*, e_F^*) = (e_L, e_L)$. Hence, in any case the winning probability of either player will be $\frac{1}{2}$, but only under low risk each one has to bear positive effort costs. Consequently, the challenger prefers high risk at stage 1 to commit himself (and his rival) to choose minimal effort at stage 2 in order to save effort costs. Concerning the cost effect, both players' interests are perfectly aligned as each one prefers a kind of implicit collusion in the tournament, induced by high risk.

The third effect arises if $\frac{c_F}{\Delta G\left(\sigma_H^2\right)} < B < \frac{c_U}{\Delta G\left(\sigma_H^2\right)}$.[5] In this situation, the outcome at the effort stage is $(e_U^*, e_F^*) = (e_L, e_H)$, no matter which risk level has been chosen at stage 1. Here, risk-taking only determines the players'

---

[4] See the proof of Proposition 2 in the Appendix.

[5] See again the proof of Proposition 2.

likelihoods of winning so that this effect is called *likelihood effect*. If F chooses risk, he will unambiguously prefer low risk $\sigma^2 = \sigma_L^2$. Higher risk-taking would shift probability mass from the mean to the tails. This is detrimental for the favorite, since bad luck may jeopardize his favorable position at the effort stage. By choosing low risk, his winning probability becomes $G\left(\Delta e; \sigma_L^2\right)$ instead of $G\left(\Delta e; \sigma_H^2\right)$ $\left(< G\left(\Delta e; \sigma_L^2\right)\right)$. A technical intuition can be seen from Figure 4.2.

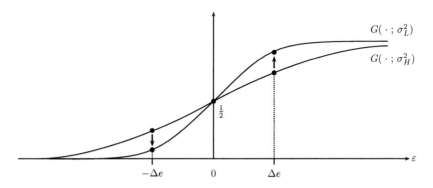

Figure 4.2: Likelihood effect

Note that at Δe the cdf describes the winning probability of player F, whereas U's likelihood of winning is computed at $-\Delta e$. Thus, by choosing low risk instead of high risk, the favorite maximizes his own winning probability and minimizes that of his opponent.

To sum up, the analysis of risk-taking by the favorite points to three different effects at the risk stage of the game. These three effects are tested in a laboratory experiment which will be described in the next section.[6] Thereafter, we will present the exact hypotheses to be tested and our experimental results.

---

[6] Note that we will not consider the case $B < \min\left\{\frac{c_F}{\Delta G(\sigma_H^2)}, \frac{c_U}{\Delta G(\sigma_L^2)}\right\}$ in the lab. Here, low risk would imply a higher winning probability at higher effort costs for the favorite. Hence, we would have a mixture of the likelihood effect and the cost effect, which would not lead to additional insights when testing in an experiment.

4.4 Experimental Design and Procedure

We designed three different treatments corresponding to our three effects – the discouragement effect, the cost effect, and the likelihood effect. For each treatment we conducted two sessions, each including five groups of six participants. Each session consisted of ten trial rounds and five rounds of the two-stage game. During each round, pairs of two players were matched anonymously within each group. After each round new pairs were matched in all groups. The game was repeated five times so that each player interacted with each other player exactly one time within a certain group. This perfect stranger matching was implemented to prevent reputation effects. Altogether, for each treatment we have 30 independent observations concerning the first round (15 pairs, two sessions) and ten independent observations based on all rounds.

Before the five rounds of each session started, each participant had the chance to become familiar with the complete two-stage game of Section 4.2 for ten rounds. During the trial rounds, a single player had to make all decisions on his own so that he learned the role of the favorite as well as that of the underdog. Within the five rounds of the experiment the participants were assigned to alternate roles. Hence, each individual either played three rounds as a favorite and two rounds as an underdog or vice versa.

In each session, the players competed for the same benefit ($B = 100$) and chose between the same alternative effort levels ($e_L = 0$ and $e_H = 1$). We used a uniformly distributed noise term ε for each session which was either distributed between -2 and 2 ("low risk"), or between -4 and 4 ("high risk").[7] Hence, we had $\Delta G\left(\sigma_L^2\right) = \frac{1}{4}$ and $\Delta G\left(\sigma_H^2\right) = \frac{1}{8}$. However, we varied the effort costs between the treatments. In the *discouragement treatment* (focusing on the discouragement effect) we used $c_U = 24$ and $c_F = 8$, in the *cost treatment* (testing the cost effect) we had $c_U = 24$ and $c_F = 22$, and in the *likelihood treatment* (dealing with the likelihood effect) we had $c_U = 60$ and $c_F = 8$. It can easily be checked that these three different parameter constellations satisfy the three different conditions for the benefit

---

[7]Random draws were rounded off to two decimal places.

corresponding to the discouragement effect, the cost effect and the likelihood effect, respectively. All parameter values B, e_L, e_H, c_U, c_F, as well as the intervals were common knowledge.

The experiment was conducted at the Cologne Laboratory of Economic Research at the University of Cologne in January 2008. Altogether, 180 students participated in the experiment. All of them were enrolled in the Faculty of Management, Economics, and Social Sciences. The participants were recruited via the online recruitment system by Greiner (2003). The experiment was programmed and conducted with the software z-tree (Fischbacher (2007)). A session approximately lasted one hour and 15 minutes and subjects earned on average 13.82 Euro.

At the outset of each session the subjects were randomly assigned to a cubicle where they took a seat in front of a computer terminal. The instructions were handed out and read aloud by the experimenters.[8] Thereafter, the subjects had time to ask clarifying questions if they had any difficulties in understanding the instructions. Communication – other than with the experimental software – was not allowed. To check for their comprehension, subjects had to answer a short questionnaire. After each of the subjects correctly solved the questions, the experimental software was started.

At the beginning of each session, the players got 60 units of the fictitious currency "Taler". Each round of the experiment then proceeded according to the two-stage game described in Section 4.2. It started with player F's risk choice at stage 1 of the game. He could either choose a random draw out of the interval $[-2, 2]$ ("low risk") or out of the interval $[-4, 4]$ ("high risk"). When choosing risk, player F knew the course of events at the next stage as well as both players' effort costs. At the beginning of stage 2, both players were informed about the interval that had been chosen by player F before. Then both players were asked about their beliefs concerning the effort choice of their respective opponent. Thereafter, each player i ($i = U, F$) chose between score 0 (at zero costs) and score 1 (at costs c_i) as alternative effort levels. Next, the random draw was executed. The final score of player F consisted of his initially chosen score 0 or 1 plus the realization of the

---

[8]The translated instructions can be found in the Appendix.

random draw, whereas the final score of player U was identical with his initially chosen score 0 or 1.[9] The player with the higher final score was the winner of this round and the other one the loser. Both players were informed about both final scores, whether the guess about the opponent's choice was correct, and about the realized payoffs. Then the next round began.

Each session ended after five rounds. At the end of the session, one of the five rounds was drawn by lot. For this round, each player got 15 Talers if his guess of the opponent's effort choice was correct and zero Talers otherwise. The winner of the selected round received $B = 100$ Talers and the loser zero Talers. Each player had to pay zero or c_i Talers for the chosen score 0 or 1, respectively. The sum of Talers was then converted into Euro by a previously known exchange rate of 1 Euro per 10 Talers. Additionally, each participant received a show up fee of 2.50 Euro independent of the game's outcome. After the final round, the subjects were requested to complete a questionnaire including questions on gender, age, loss aversion and inequity aversion. Furthermore, the questionnaire contained questions concerning the risk attitude of the subjects. Again these questions were taken from the German Socio Economic Panel (GSOEP) and dealt with the overall risk attitude of a subject.

The language was kept neutral at any time. For example, we did not use terms like "favorite" and "underdog", or "player F" and "player U", but instead spoke of "player A" and "player B". Moreover, we simply described the pure random draw out of the two alternative intervals without speaking of low or high risk. Instead favorites chose between "alternative 1" and "alternative 2".

4.5 Hypotheses

We test seven hypotheses, six of them deal with the risk behavior and one of them with the players' behavior at the effort stage.

The first three hypotheses directly test the relevance of the discourage-

---

[9]Hence, the relative performance RP is given by the final score of player F minus the final score of player U.

ment effect, the cost effect and the likelihood effect at stage 1 of the game. Since we designed three different constellations by changing one of the cost parameters, respectively, each effect can be separately analyzed in a single treatment. The cost treatment is obtained from the discouragement treatment by increasing the favorite's cost parameter, whereas the design of the likelihood treatment results from increasing the underdog's cost parameter in the discouragement treatment.

Hypothesis 1: *In the discouragement treatment, (most of) the favorites choose the high risk.*

Hypothesis 2: *In the cost treatment, (most of) the favorites choose the high risk.*

Hypothesis 3: *In the likelihood treatment, (most of) the favorites choose the low risk.*

In a next step, we compare the risk choices in the different treatments. We expect that risk-taking clearly differs among the three treatments. The corresponding behavioral hypotheses can be described as follows:

Hypothesis 4: *The favorites' risk-taking in the cost treatment does not differ from that in the discouragement treatment.*[10]

Hypothesis 5: *The favorites choose higher risk in the discouragement treatment than in the likelihood treatment.*

Hypothesis 6: *The favorites choose higher risk in the cost treatment than in the likelihood treatment.*

Finally, we test the players' effort choices at the second stage of the game. Since in any equilibrium at the effort stage the favorite should not choose less effort than the underdog, we have the following hypothesis:

---

[10]Of course, we cannot test whether risk taking is identical in both treatments, but we can test whether significant differences between the treatments do exist.

Hypothesis 7: *The favorites choose at least as much effort as the underdogs.*[11]

4.6 Experimental Results

4.6.1 The Risk Stage

We test the hypotheses with the data from our experiment, starting with Hypotheses 1 to 3. Contrary to the discouragement treatment, the findings on the favorites' risk choices in the cost and the likelihood treatments are in line with our theoretical predictions on average (see Figure 4.3 and Table 4.4 in the Appendix): favorites tend to choose high risk (low risk) more often than low risk (high risk) in the cost treatment (likelihood treatment). However, when applying the one-tailed Binomial test we cannot reject the hypothesis that favorites randomly choose between high and low risk in the cost treatment in the first round. To check whether we can pool the data over all rounds, we run different regressions (see Tables 4.5 to 4.7 in the Appendix). As the subjects play the game five times, we compute robust standard errors clustered by subjects and check for learning effects by including round dummies. In contrast to the previous chapters we do not find any significant learning effects over time in all treatments since there is no significant influence of a certain round on risk-taking. Additionally, we compare risk-taking in round one with the risk-taking of rounds two to five for each treatment but do not find significant differences. We think that the relatively large number of ten trial rounds at the beginning of the experiment help the subjects to study the consequences of different strategies. If there are any learning effects, these should only be relevant in this trial phase. Thus, we pool our data over the five rounds. In the following we present the results of the first round and additionally our results with pooled data.

---

[11] Our hypotheses are stated in terms of "higher" risk and effort, but tests will deal with the frequency of the appearance of the two risk and effort levels. However, the interpretation does not change. If we observe, for example, that there is a significant higher proportion of favorites than underdogs choosing the high effort level, this also means that the average effort chosen by the favorites is higher.

The results of the one-tailed Binomial tests concerning Hypotheses 1 to 3 are summarized in Table 4.1.[12]

risk choice	discouragement treatment	cost treatment	likelihood treatment
first round	high risk	high risk	low risk**
pooled data	high risk	high risk	low risk***

($^*0.05 < \alpha \leq 0.10$; $^{**}0.01 < \alpha \leq 0.05$; $^{***}\alpha \leq 0.01$)

Table 4.1: Results on risk-taking (one-tailed Binomial tests)

Observation on Hypothesis 1 − 3: *Favorites more often choose low risk than high risk in the likelihood treatment, whereas the findings on high risk-taking in the discouragement and the cost treatments are not significant.*

In a next step, we compare the three treatments pairwise.

Observation on Hypothesis 4: *Favorites' risk-taking in the cost treatment significantly differs from that in the discouragement treatment.* (Fisher test, two-tailed; first round: $p = 0.008$; pooled data: $p = 0.000$)

Whereas the Binomial test shows that favorites do not prefer high risk significantly stronger than low risk in the cost treatment, the relative comparison supports the initial impression from Figure 4.3: in the cost treatment, the proportion of favorites choosing the high risk is higher than in the discouragement treatment so that Hypothesis 4 can be clearly rejected. Therefore, the cost effect seems to be more relevant for subjects when choosing risk than the discouragement effect. In addition, we run a probit regression with the risk choice as the dependent variable, using our pooled data set (see Table 4.5 in the Appendix). Here, the dummy variable for the cost treatment is highly significant which confirms our result from the Fisher test.

---

[12]Table entries indicate the predicted risk choices.

Observation on Hypothesis 5: *Favorites' risk-taking in the discouragement treatment is not significantly higher than that in the likelihood treatment* (one-tailed Fisher test).

The observation on Hypothesis 5 holds for the first round as well as for the pooled data set and is in line with our previous findings: in the likelihood treatment, favorites choose low risk as theoretically expected. Since, contrary to theory, they also often choose low risk in the discouragement treatment, risk-taking is not significantly higher in the discouragement treatment. Again, we run a probit regression with the pooled data, but do not find a significant result for the treatment dummy (see Table 4.6 in the Appendix).

Observation on Hypothesis 6: *Favorites' risk-taking is significantly higher in the cost treatment than in the likelihood treatment* (Fisher test, one-tailed; first round: $p = 0.018$; pooled data: $p = 0.000$)

Again, the Fisher test supports the general impression of Figure 4.3: favorites choose significantly higher risk in the cost treatment compared to the risk behavior in the likelihood treatment. Further confirmation comes from a respective probit regression (see Table 4.7 in the Appendix). Note that all three probit regressions show that risk aversion does not have a significant influence on the favorites' risk-taking.

4.6.2 The Effort Stage

Given the favorite's risk choice at stage 1, the underdog and the favorite have to decide on their efforts at the second stage of the game. According to the subgame perfect equilibria, we would expect that the favorite chooses a higher effort level than the underdog in the discouragement and the likelihood treatments, whereas both players' efforts should be the same in the cost treatment. Altogether, favorites should exert more effort than underdogs on average.[13]

---

[13]Uneven tournaments in the notion of O'Keeffe et al. (1984) are also considered in the experiments by Bull et al. (1987), Schotter and Weigelt (1992) and Harbring et al. (2007).

Recall that in the discouragement and the cost treatments different risk levels lead to different equilibria at the effort stage. Since both risk levels have been chosen at stage 1, we can test whether players react rationally to a given risk level. An overview on the aggregate effort choices is given by Figures 4.4 to 4.12 and Tables 4.8 to 4.16 in the Appendix: in the discouragement treatment, the favorite should always choose the large effort level independent of given risk, whereas the underdog should prefer small (large) effort if risk is high (low). Figures 4.4 to 4.6 show that the experimental findings are roughly in line with our theoretical predictions. For high risk, the subjects even perfectly react to given risk in round five – all underdogs choose low effort, but all favorites prefer the high effort level. In the cost treatment, theory predicts that both types of players choose small efforts under high risk, but large efforts under low risk which is in line with our results from Chapter 3. Figures 4.7 to 4.9 illustrate that subjects on average indeed react as predicted. Interestingly, favorites are more sensitive to risk than underdogs although subjects change their roles after each round. In the likelihood treatment, for both risk levels favorites (underdogs) should choose large (small) effort. As for the risk stage, in the likelihood treatment subjects' behavior seems to follow theoretical predictions also most closely when choosing effort, compared to the other treatments (see Figures 4.10 to 4.12).

Next, we used a one-tailed Binomial test to check if most of the subjects of a certain type choose the predicted effort level under a given risk against the hypothesis that subjects randomly decide between the two effort levels. Again, we can pool our data over the five rounds because regressions including round dummies (see Tables 4.17 to 4.19 in the Appendix) as well as tests comparing the effort in round 1 with the effort of rounds 2 to 5 for a particular type and particular risk do not reveal any significant learning effects at the effort stage. Table 4.2 presents all first-round observations and the results for pooled data (a table entry illustrates the predicted effort level). The column corresponding to the discouragement treatment reveals that favorites' reactions to risk-taking are quite in line with theory as they choose

---

In each experiment, favorites choose significantly higher effort levels than underdogs.

high efforts for both risk levels. However, the underdogs' behavior is not significantly different from a random draw under low risk, but in line with the theoretical prediction under high risk (first round: $p = 0.0625$, pooled: $p = 0.0004$).

	player: data	discouragement treatment	cost treatment	likelihood treatment
high risk	F: 1ˢᵗ round	$e_F = 1$	$e_F = 0^{**}$	$e_F = 1$
	F: pooled	$e_F = 1^{***}$	$e_F = 0^{***}$	$e_F = 1^{***}$
	U: 1ˢᵗ round	$e_U = 0^*$	$e_U = 0$	$e_U = 0^{**}$
	U: pooled	$e_U = 0^{***}$	$e_U = 0$	$e_U = 0^{***}$
low risk	F: 1ˢᵗ round	$e_F = 1^{***}$	$e_F = 1$	$e_F = 1^{***}$
	F: pooled	$e_F = 1^{***}$	$e_F = 1^{***}$	$e_F = 1^{***}$
	U: 1ˢᵗ round	$e_U = 1$	$e_U = 1^*$	$e_U = 0^*$
	U: pooled	$e_U = 1$	$e_U = 1^{**}$	$e_U = 0^{***}$

($^*0.05 < \alpha \leq 0.10$; $^{**}0.01 < \alpha \leq 0.05$; $^{***}\alpha \leq 0.01$)

Table 4.2: Results on effort choices (One-tailed Binomial tests)

The column for the cost treatment confirms the initial impression from Figures 4.7 to 4.9. Whereas favorites react fairly well to different risk levels, the underdogs often choose high effort even under high risk, which contradicts theory. The last column reports the findings for the likelihood treatment. Our results point out that subjects behave rationally at the effort stage with the exception of the favorites' effort choices in the first round given high risk.

Finally, we test the favorites' effort choices against the underdogs' behavior (compare Table 4.3). We either used a one-tailed Fisher test to check if the proportion of favorites choosing the high effort is significantly larger than that of the underdogs if theory predicts a higher effort level of the favorite ($e_F > e_U$), or a two-tailed Fisher test to check if there are any (unpredicted) differences between the proportion of types in the two effort categories. We have differentiated between three cases when comparing efforts – ignoring the given risk level (first panel of the table), only considering high-risk situations (second panel), and only considering low-risk situations (third panel). Following the theoretical predictions, in the discouragement treatment favorites should only exert more effort than underdogs if risk is high.

	data	discouragement treatment	cost treatment	likelihood treatment
both risks	1st round	one-tailed***	two-tailed	one-tailed***
	pooled	one-tailed***	two-tailed	one-tailed***
high risk	1st round	one-tailed*	two-tailed	one-tailed**
	pooled	one-tailed***	two-tailed***	one-tailed***
low risk	1st round	two-tailed	two-tailed	one-tailed***
	pooled	two-tailed***	two-tailed	one-tailed***

($^*0.05 < \alpha \leq 0.10$; $^{**}0.01 < \alpha \leq 0.05$; $^{***}\alpha \leq 0.01$)

Table 4.3: Results on effort comparisons (Fisher test)

The second panel of the table fits well with this prediction for the first round ($p = 0.051$) and pooled data ($p = 0.000$), but according to the third panel subjects' behavior seems to be different even under low risk: considering the pooled data, favorites choose a significantly different effort than underdogs ($p = 0.000$), thus contradicting theory. Inspecting the data reveals that the proportion of favorites choosing the high effort is even significantly higher than the respective proportion of underdogs under low risk. In both the cost treatment and the likelihood treatment, the effort difference $e_F - e_U$ should be independent of the risk level. $e_F - e_U$ should be zero under the cost treatment, but strictly positive under the likelihood treatment. Again, the findings for the likelihood treatment are mostly in line with theory. For the cost treatment, the second panel of the table shows that the different types of players choose significantly different effort levels under high risk (pooled data: $p = 0.001$). Here, the underdogs exert clearly more effort than the favorites which is in line with our observations in Figures 4.7 and 4.9 and the findings for the Binomial test, but contrary to theory.

Finally, we run probit regressions on the effort comparison between favorites and underdogs for the three different treatments (see Tables 4.17 to 4.19 in the Appendix). The regression results clearly support our findings for the Fisher test: whereas the player-type dummy is (highly) significant and in line with theory for the discouragement and the likelihood treatments, it is not significant or even significantly different from theoretical predictions in the cost treatment. Furthermore, we check if a player's risk attitude influences his behavior at the effort stage. None of the regressions show a significant influence of the risk attitude of the player on his choice of effort.

Hence, we can summarize our findings for the effort stage as follows:

Observation on Hypothesis 7: *In the discouragement treatment and the likelihood treatment, favorites choose significantly more effort than underdogs. In the cost treatment, players' behavior does not significantly differ given low risk, but for high risk underdogs exert clearly more effort than favorites.*

4.7 Discussion

The experimental results of Section 4.6 point to three puzzles, which should be discussed in the following: (1) favorites choose significantly more often the low risk than the high risk in the discouragement treatment; (2) given low risk in the discouragement treatment, favorites exert significantly more effort than underdogs; (3) given high risk in the cost treatment, underdogs choose significantly more effort than favorites.

Inspection of the players' beliefs concerning their opponents' efforts shows that puzzles (1) and (2) seem to be interrelated. It turns out that in the low-risk state of the discouragement treatment, favorites' equilibrium beliefs differ from their reported beliefs in each of the five rounds of the repeated game. In the first and in the last round, 11 out of 23 favorites expect underdogs to choose a low effort level although theory predicts a high effort choice. The proportion of favorites with this belief is even higher in round two (10 out of 18), round three (10 out of 20) and round four (12 out of 21). Actually, about one half of the underdogs choose a low effort. Given that the favorites already have these beliefs when taking risk at stage 1, both puzzles (1) and

(2) can be easily explained together: now, a favorite expecting a low effort by an underdog in both a low-risk and a high-risk state should unambiguously prefer a high effort level in both states. The results of our Binomial test from Subsection 4.6.1 show that indeed favorites react in this way with a high significance. This explains puzzle (2). When the favorites decide on risk-taking at stage 1 and anticipate $(e_U, e_F) = (0, 1)$ under both risks, the underlying discouragement problem turns into a perceived likelihood problem from the viewpoint of the favorites.[14] Given a perceived likelihood problem, the favorites should optimally choose a low risk in order to maximize their winning probability (see Figure 4.2), which explains puzzle (1).

Concerning puzzle (3), inspection of the players' beliefs does not lead to clear results. Similarly, controlling for risk aversion, loss aversion, inequity aversion and the history of the game does not yield new insights either. Most surprisingly seems to be the missing explanatory power of the players' history in the game: intuitively, subjects might react to the outcomes of former rounds when choosing effort in the actual round. However, our results do not show a clear impact of experienced success or failure in previous tournaments. Maybe underdogs react too strongly to the close competition with the favorites. In the cost treatment, costs for exerting high effort were $c_U = 24$ and $c_F = 22$. Hence, the cost difference is rather small – in particular compared to the two other treatments –, and the underdogs might have chosen high efforts due to perceived homogeneity in the tournament. The underdogs' beliefs about the favorites' effort choices indicate that this effect might be relevant under high risk. In the first and third round, seven (out of 18 and 15 respectively), and in the fourth round eight (out of 19) underdogs expect favorites to choose high efforts, too.[15] However, in the concrete situation given $\sigma^2 = \sigma_H^2$ and $e_F = 1$, an underdog should prefer $e_U = 1$ to $e_U = 0$ if and only if $\frac{B}{2} - c_U > B \cdot G(-\Delta e; \sigma_H^2) \Leftrightarrow B \cdot \Delta G(\sigma_H^2) > c_U$, and for our chosen parameter values this condition (12.5 Talers > 24 Talers) is clearly violated.[16] As we have seen in Chapter 3 players base their effort decision

---

[14] See also the observation on Hypothesis 5 in Subsection 4.6.1.

[15] In the other two rounds the proportion of underdogs who believe the favorite to choose the high effort is somewhat lower: second round: 3 out of 13; last round: 4 out of 17.

[16] Note that in terms of converted money payments, subjects have to compare 1.25 Euro

solely on their own choice of risk in the case of bilateral risk-taking. Therefore, the favorites might respond stronger to the chosen risk because it was
their own choice whereas the underdogs have to take risk as given. To sum
up, as we can see from Figures 4.7 and 4.8, underdogs reduce their efforts
when risk increases, which is qualitatively in line with the cost effect, but
it remains puzzling why underdogs do not react as strongly as favorites to
different risks although subjects changed their roles after each round in the
experiment.

4.8 Conclusion

In many winner-take-all situations, a challenger first decides whether to use
a more or less risky strategy and then both players choose their investments
or efforts. In this case, risk-taking at the first stage of the game determines
both the optimal investment or effort levels at stage two and the players'
likelihood of winning the competition. We find three effects that mainly
determine risk-taking – a discouragement effect, a cost effect, and a likelihood
effect. Our experimental findings point out that the impact of risk-taking
on the likelihood of winning (i.e. the likelihood effect) is very important
for subjects at stage one. Moreover, optimal investments for given risk are
clearly in line with theory under the likelihood effect. Furthermore, in most
of the rounds even the beliefs of the favorites seem to follow the theoretical
beliefs in the likelihood treatment. In addition, the beliefs of the underdogs
are in line with the theory in all rounds. We obtain mixed results for the cost
effect and the discouragement effect, but pairwise comparison of treatments
reveals that the cost effect seems to be more relevant for subjects than the
discouragement effect. Interestingly, the players very often react to given risk
according to theory when investing into the winner-take-all competition.

As a by-product, the results of our questionnaire point to an important finding on the concept of inequity aversion[17] as introduced by Fehr and

---

to 2.40 Euro. Given $e_F = 0$, high effort would only be rational for the underdog if 1.25
Euro > 2.40 Euro which is clearly not satisfied.

[17]We use the same two games as Dannenberg et al. (2007) to measure the subjects'

Schmidt (1999) in the literature. Grund and Sliwka (2005) applied this concept to rank-order tournaments. If one player has a higher (lower) payoff than another player, the first (second) realizes a disutility from compassion (envy). In a tournament, players typically compare their relative payoffs and the tournament winner (loser) will feel some compassion (envy) when being inequity averse. Both Fehr and Schmidt (1999) and Grund and Sliwka (2005) assume that envy is at least as strong as compassion. This assumption is central for the results in Grund and Sliwka (2005) since it directly implies that inequity averse contestants exert more effort than players who are not inequity averse. Using a sign test,[18] our findings point out that in each treatment subjects feel significantly more compassion than envy (one-tailed, discouragement treatment: $p = 0.000$, cost treatment: $p = 0.000$, likelihood treatment: $p = 0.000$).[19] According to this result, inequity aversion would not lead to stronger competition in tournaments. On the contrary, competition would be weakened as any contestant anticipates to suffer from strong compassion in case of winning.

---

inequity preferences. In contrast to Dannenberg et al. (2007), not all subjects received a payoff for their decisions. After the subjects indicated their decisions, we randomly determined for which game and which row of that particular game two randomly selected subjects received a payoff according to their decisions. Furthermore, the respective player role of the selected subjects was randomly determined.

[18] Subjects with inconsistent behavior were excluded from the analysis.

[19] A similar finding is made by Dannenberg et al. (2007) running experiments on public good games.

4.9 Appendix to Chapter 4

Proof of Proposition 2:

(i) We can rewrite 4.6 as

$$(e_U^*, e_F^*) = \begin{cases} (e_H, e_H) & \text{if } B \geq \frac{c_U}{\Delta G(\sigma^2)} \\ (e_L, e_H) & \text{if } \frac{c_U}{\Delta G(\sigma^2)} \geq B \geq \frac{c_F}{\Delta G(\sigma^2)} \\ (e_L, e_L) & \text{if } B \leq \frac{c_F}{\Delta G(\sigma^2)}. \end{cases} \tag{4.7}$$

Since we have two risk levels, σ_L^2 and σ_H^2, there are four cutoffs with $\frac{c_F}{\Delta G(\sigma_H^2)}$ being the smallest one and $\frac{c_U}{\Delta G(\sigma_H^2)}$ the largest one because of 4.5. Hence, both players will always (never) choose high effort levels if $B \geq \frac{c_U}{\Delta G(\sigma_H^2)}$ ($B \leq \frac{c_F}{\Delta G(\sigma_L^2)}$), irrespective of risk-taking in stage 1.

(ii) We have to differentiate between two possible rankings of the cutoffs:

$$\text{scenario 1:} \quad \frac{c_F}{\Delta G\left(\sigma_L^2\right)} < \frac{c_F}{\Delta G\left(\sigma_H^2\right)} < \frac{c_U}{\Delta G\left(\sigma_L^2\right)} < \frac{c_U}{\Delta G\left(\sigma_H^2\right)}$$

$$\text{scenario 2:} \quad \frac{c_F}{\Delta G\left(\sigma_L^2\right)} < \frac{c_U}{\Delta G\left(\sigma_L^2\right)} < \frac{c_F}{\Delta G\left(\sigma_H^2\right)} < \frac{c_U}{\Delta G\left(\sigma_H^2\right)}.$$

If $B < \min\left\{\frac{c_F}{\Delta G(\sigma_H^2)}, \frac{c_U}{\Delta G(\sigma_L^2)}\right\}$, then in both scenarios the choice of σ_L^2 will imply $(e_U^*, e_F^*) = (e_L, e_H)$ at stage 2, whereas $\sigma^2 = \sigma_H^2$ will lead to $(e_U^*, e_F^*) = (e_L, e_L)$. In this situation, a F-challenger prefers $\sigma^2 = \sigma_L^2$ since

$$B \cdot G\left(\Delta e; \sigma_L^2\right) - c_F > \frac{B}{2} \Leftrightarrow B > \frac{c_F}{\Delta G\left(\sigma_L^2\right)}$$

is true. However, a U-challenger prefers $\sigma^2 = \sigma_H^2$ because of

$$\frac{B}{2} > B \cdot G\left(-\Delta e; \sigma_L^2\right).$$

If $B > \max\left\{\frac{c_F}{\Delta G(\sigma_H^2)}, \frac{c_U}{\Delta G(\sigma_L^2)}\right\}$, then in both scenarios the choice of σ_L^2 will result into $(e_U^*, e_F^*) = (e_H, e_H)$ at stage 2, but $\sigma^2 = \sigma_H^2$ will induce $(e_U^*, e_F^*) =$

(e_L, e_H). In this case, a F-challenger prefers the high risk σ_H^2 since

$$B \cdot G\left(\Delta e; \sigma_H^2\right) - c_F > \frac{B}{2} - c_F.$$

Player U has the same preference when being the challenger because

$$B \cdot G\left(-\Delta e; \sigma_H^2\right) > \frac{B}{2} - c_U \Leftrightarrow \frac{c_U}{\Delta G\left(\sigma_H^2\right)} > B$$

is true.

Two cases are still missing. Under scenario 1, we may have that

$$\frac{c_F}{\Delta G\left(\sigma_H^2\right)} < B < \frac{c_U}{\Delta G\left(\sigma_L^2\right)}.$$

Then any risk choice leads to $(e_U^*, e_F^*) = (e_L, e_H)$ at stage 2 and a F-challenger prefers σ_L^2 because of

$$B \cdot G\left(\Delta e; \sigma_L^2\right) - c_F > B \cdot G\left(\Delta e; \sigma_H^2\right) - c_F,$$

but U favors σ_H^2 when being active at stage 1 since

$$B \cdot G\left(-\Delta e; \sigma_H^2\right) > B \cdot G\left(-\Delta e; \sigma_L^2\right).$$

Under scenario 2, we may have that

$$\frac{c_U}{\Delta G\left(\sigma_L^2\right)} < B < \frac{c_F}{\Delta G\left(\sigma_H^2\right)}.$$

Here, low risk σ_L^2 implies $(e_U^*, e_F^*) = (e_H, e_H)$, but high risk σ_H^2 leads to $(e_U^*, e_F^*) = (e_L, e_L)$. Obviously, each type of challenger prefers the choice of high risk at stage 1. Our findings are summarized in Proposition 2 (ii). ∎

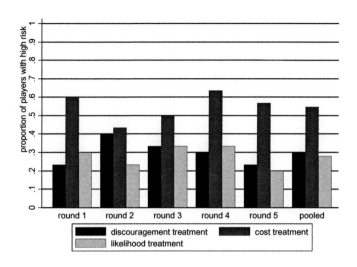

Figure 4.3: Comparison of the favorite's risk choices over treatments

Treatment	Round 1	Round 2	Round 3	Round 4	Round 5	Pooled
Discourage	7	12	10	9	7	45
Cost	18	13	15	19	17	82
Likelihood	9	7	10	10	6	42

Table 4.4: Comparison of the favorite's risk choices over treatments: Number of players choosing high risk, $n = 30$ for rounds $1 - 5$ and $n = 150$ for pooled data

	(1)	(2)
Dummy cost treatment	0.6430***	0.6310***
	(0.20)	(0.20)
Risk attitude		−0.0398
		(0.044)
Dummy round 2	0.0085	0.0061
	(0.24)	(0.24)
Dummy round 3	0.0052	0.0133
	(0.20)	(0.20)
Dummy round 4	0.1360	0.1280
	(0.17)	(0.17)
Dummy round 5	−0.0449	−0.0401
	(0.21)	(0.22)
Constant	−0.5460***	−0.3490
	(0.19)	(0.29)
Observations	300	300
Pseudo R^2	0.0479	0.0514
Pseudo Loglikelihood	−194.61582	−193.89994

Robust standard errors in parentheses are calculated by clustering on subjects
***$p < 0.01$, **$p < 0.05$, *$p < 0.10$

Table 4.5: Probit regression Hypothesis 4: Comparison of the favorite's risk-taking in the cost and discouragement treatment

	(1)	(2)
Dummy likelihood treatment	−0.0584	−0.0561
	(0.22)	(0.22)
Risk attitude		0.0125
		(0.05)
Dummy round 2	0.1450	0.1470
	(0.24)	(0.24)
Dummy round 3	0.1920	0.1900
	(0.19)	(0.19)
Dummy round 4	0.1460	0.1490
	(0.19)	(0.19)
Dummy round 5	−0.1610	−0.1640
	(0.23)	(0.23)
Constant	−0.5930***	−0.6570**
	(0.20)	(0.32)
Observations	300	300
Pseudo R^2	0.0080	0.0084
Pseudo Loglikelihood	−179.19263	−179.17939

Robust standard errors in parentheses are calculated by clustering on subjects
***$p < 0.01$, **$p < 0.05$, *$p < 0.10$

Table 4.6: Probit regression Hypothesis 5: Comparison of the favorite's risk-taking in the discouragement and the likelihood treatment

	(1)	(2)
Dummy cost treatment	0.707***	0.708***
	(0.21)	(0.21)
Risk attitude		0.006
		(0.047)
Dummy round 2	−0.321	−0.318
	(0.24)	(0.24)
Dummy round 3	−0.087	−0.086
	(0.19)	(0.19)
Dummy round 4	0.090	0.091
	(0.17)	(0.17)
Dummy round 5	−0.186	−0.184
	(0.21)	(0.21)
Constant	−0.488**	−0.516*
	(0.20)	(0.29)
Observations	300	300
Pseudo R^2	0.0637	0.0638
Pseudo Loglikelihood	−190.44806	−190.43411

Robust standard errors in parentheses are calculated by clustering on subjects
***$p < 0.01$, **$p < 0.05$, *$p < 0.10$

Table 4.7: Probit regression Hypothesis 6: Comparison of the favorite's risk-taking in the cost and likelihood treatment

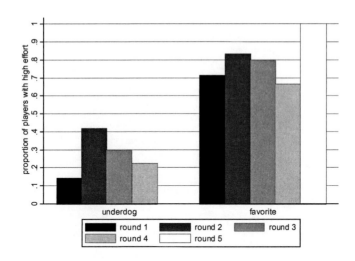

Figure 4.4: Effort choices in the discouragement treatment with high risk

	Round 1	Round 2	Round 3	Round 4	Round 5
Underdog	1 of 7	5 of 12	3 of 10	2 of 9	0 of 7
Favorite	5 of 7	10 of 12	8 of 10	6 of 9	7 of 7

Table 4.8: Effort choices in the discouragement treatment with high risk: Number of players choosing high effort

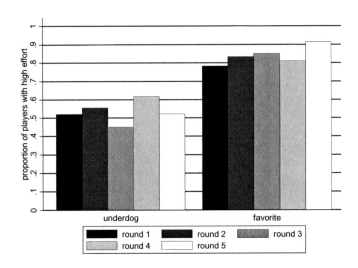

Figure 4.5: Effort choices in the discouragement treatment with low risk

	Round 1	Round 2	Round 3	Round 4	Round 5
Underdog	12 of 23	10 of 18	9 of 20	13 of 21	12 of 23
Favorite	18 of 23	15 of 18	17 of 20	17 of 21	21 of 23

Table 4.9: Effort choices in the discouragement treatment with low risk: Number of players choosing high effort

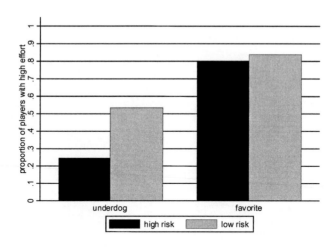

Figure 4.6: Effort choices in the discouragement treatment with pooled data

	High risk	Low risk
Underdog	11 of 45	56 of 105
Favorite	36 of 45	88 of 105

Table 4.10: Effort choices in the discouragement treatment with pooled data: Number of players choosing high effort

115

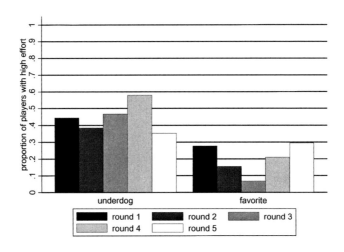

Figure 4.7: Effort choices in the cost treatment with high risk

	Round 1	Round 2	Round 3	Round 4	Round 5
Underdog	8 of 18	5 of 13	7 of 15	11 of 19	6 of 17
Favorite	5 of 18	2 of 13	1 of 15	4 of 19	5 of 17

Table 4.11: Effort choices in the cost treatment with high risk: Number of players choosing high effort

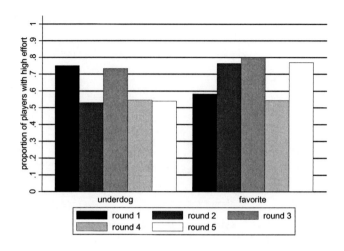

Figure 4.8: Effort choices in the cost treatment with low risk

	Round 1	Round 2	Round 3	Round 4	Round 5
Underdog	9 of 12	9 of 17	11 of 15	6 of 11	7 of 13
Favorite	7 of 12	13 of 17	12 of 15	6 of 11	10 of 13

Table 4.12: Effort choices in the cost treatment with low risk: Number of players choosing high effort

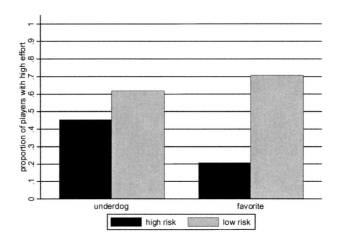

Figure 4.9: Effort choices in the cost treatment with pooled data

	High risk	Low risk
Underdog	37 of 82	42 of 68
Favorite	17 of 82	48 of 68

Table 4.13: Effort choices in the cost treatment with pooled data: Number of players choosing high effort

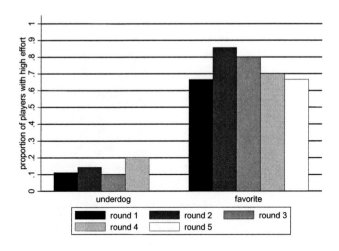

Figure 4.10: Effort choices in the likelihood treatment with high risk

	Round 1	Round 2	Round 3	Round 4	Round 5
Underdog	1 of 9	1 of 7	1 of 10	2 of 10	0 of 6
Favorite	6 of 9	6 of 7	8 of 10	7 of 10	4 of 6

Table 4.14: Effort choices in the likelihood treatment with high risk: Number of players choosing high effort

119

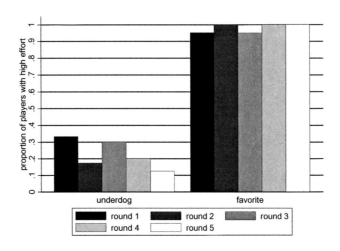

Figure 4.11: Effort choices in the likelihood treatment with low risk

	Round 1	Round 2	Round 3	Round 4	Round 5
Underdog	7 of 21	4 of 23	6 of 20	4 of 20	3 of 24
Favorite	20 of 21	23 of 23	19 of 20	20 of 20	24 of 24

Table 4.15: Effort choices in the likelihood treatment with low risk: Number of players choosing high effort

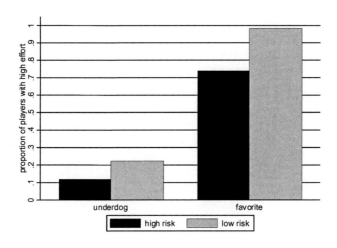

Figure 4.12: Effort choices in the likelihood treatment with pooled data

	High risk	Low risk
Underdog	5 of 42	24 of 108
Favorite	31 of 42	106 of 108

Table 4.16: Effort choices in the likelihood treatment with pooled data: Number of players choosing high effort

	High risk	High risk	Low risk	Low risk
Dummy favorite	1.580***	1.611***	0.907***	0.889***
	(0.33)	(0.33)	(0.25)	(0.25)
Risk attitude		0.048		0.053
		(0.098)		(0.071)
Dummy round 2	0.664	0.630	0.132	0.148
	(0.46)	(0.45)	(0.27)	(0.27)
Dummy round 3	0.415	0.425	0.004	−0.004
	(0.39)	(0.39)	(0.21)	(0.21)
Dummy round 4	0.064	0.034	0.186	0.193
	(0.50)	(0.50)	(0.20)	(0.20)
Dummy round 5	0.247	0.233	0.220	0.226
	(0.40)	(0.39)	(0.23)	(0.23)
Constant	−1.037***	−1.276*	−0.025	−0.278
	(0.38)	(0.67)	(0.22)	(0.40)
Observations	90	90	210	210
Pseudo R^2	0.2600	0.2640	0.0931	0.1006
Pseudo Loglikelihood	−46.09841	−45.84765	−118.55264	−117.5752

Robust standard errors in parentheses are calculated by clustering on subjects
***$p < 0.01$, **$p < 0.05$, *$p < 0.10$

Table 4.17: Probit regression Hypothesis 7: Discouragement treatment

	High risk	High risk	Low risk	Low risk
Dummy favorite	−0.704***	−0.702***	0.247	0.231
	(0.20)	(0.21)	(0.23)	(0.23)
Risk attitude		0.049		0.090
		(0.072)		(0.066)
Dummy round 2	−0.281	−0.279	−0.046	−0.032
	(0.30)	(0.31)	(0.31)	(0.32)
Dummy round 3	−0.306	−0.315	0.304	0.352
	(0.27)	(0.28)	(0.30)	(0.30)
Dummy round 4	0.086	0.079	−0.314	−0.315
	(0.22)	(0.22)	(0.34)	(0.34)
Dummy round 5	−0.101	−0.113	−0.028	0.013
	(0.27)	(0.28)	(0.28)	(0.29)
Constant	−0.022	−0.237	0.306	−0.126
	(0.25)	(0.40)	(0.26)	(0.40)
Observations	164	164	136	136
Pseudo R^2	0.0641	0.0691	0.0235	0.0395
Pseudo Loglikelihood	−97.25642	−96.73988	−84.97257	−83.57997

Robust standard errors in parentheses are calculated by clustering on subjects
***$p < 0.01$, **$p < 0.05$, *$p < 0.10$

Table 4.18: Probit regression Hypothesis 7: Cost treatment

	High risk	High risk	Low risk	Low risk
Dummy favorite	1.859***	1.907***	2.856***	2.868***
	(0.35)	(0.35)	(0.36)	(0.35)
Risk attitude		−0.082		−0.027
		(0.088)		(0.061)
Dummy round 2	0.422	0.553	−0.236	−0.230
	(0.51)	(0.46)	(0.38)	(0.38)
Dummy round 3	0.223	0.274	−0.092	−0.093
	(0.44)	(0.41)	(0.35)	(0.35)
Dummy round 4	0.240	0.292	−0.160	−0.161
	(0.53)	(0.53)	(0.31)	(0.31)
Dummy round 5	−0.265	−0.171	−0.385	−0.391
	(0.45)	(0.41)	(0.40)	(0.40)
Constant	−1.352***	−1.022*	−0.592*	−0.469
	(0.44)	(0.62)	(0.31)	(0.40)
Observations	84	84	216	216
Pseudo R^2	0.3259	0.3379	0.5415	0.5424
Pseudo Loglikelihood	−38.67116	−37.98143	−66.57126	−66.43940

Robust standard errors in parentheses are calculated by clustering on subjects
***$p < 0.01$, **$p < 0.05$, *$p < 0.10$

Table 4.19: Probit regression Hypothesis 7: Likelihood treatment

Instructions (here: for the discouragement treatment):

Welcome to this experiment!

You are taking part in an economic decision making experiment. All decisions are anonymous, that means that none of the other participants gets to know the identity of someone having made a certain decision. The payment is also anonymous, that is none of the participants gets to know how much others have earned. Please read the instructions of the experiment carefully. If you do not understand something, look at the instructions again. If you are still having questions then give us a hand signal.

Overview about the experiment

The experiment consists of five rounds. Before the experiment starts, you have the possibility to get familiar with it in ten trial rounds. These trial rounds have no influence on your payment and conduce to a better understanding of the experiment.

Each round consists of two stages: **Stage 1 and Stage 2**. In each round of the experiment you play together with a second person. All participants are divided into groups of six persons, out of which pairs for one round are chosen. If you have played together with a particular person in one round, you cannot meet this person in any further round again. Please notice that you are **only paid for one of the five rounds**. The computer randomly selects the round for which you are paid. Therefore, please think carefully about your decisions because each round might be selected. Your decisions and the decisions of the other person with whom you play influence your payment. All payments resulting of the experiment are described in the fictitious currency Taler. The **exchange rate is 1 Euro for 10 Talers**.

In the beginning of the experiment, an amount of 60 Talers will be credited to your experiment account. If you get further payments out of the randomly selected round, they will be added to your account and the whole sum will be paid out. If your payoff from the selected round is negative, it will be offset with your initial payment.

In the experiment there are two different player roles, player **role A** (player A in the following) and player **role B** (player B in the following). In the beginning, you are randomly assigned to one of these roles. In each round, you can be assigned to another role. You are then playing with a person who has the other player role. For both persons **a score is counted at the end of each round**. The player's score, depending on the player role, is influenced by several components which are presented in the following:

In case of player A:

Your score at the end of a round (after stage 2) is calculated as following:

$$\text{Score } \mathbf{A} = \mathbf{Z}_A + \mathbf{x}$$

$\mathbf{Z}_A$ is a number that you select as player A in stage 2. You can choose between $\mathbf{Z}_A = \mathbf{0}$ and $\mathbf{Z}_A = \mathbf{1}$. The selected value will be taken into account for the calculation of your score. Dependent on the choice of $\mathbf{Z}_A$, several costs occur: If you choose $Z_A = 0$, this costs you nothing. If you choose $Z_A = 1$, this costs you $\mathbf{C}_A = \mathbf{8}$ Talers.

Influence of x:
As **player A** you decide between **two alternatives** at **stage 1**:

Alternative 1:
If you choose **alternative 1**, x is randomly selected out of the interval from -2 to 2 (each value between -2 and 2 has the same probability). The randomly chosen x is specified on two decimal places.

Alternative 2:
If you choose **alternative 2**, x is randomly selected out the interval from -4 to 4 (each value between -4 and 4 has the same probability). The randomly chosen x is specified on two decimal places.
The randomly selected x influences your score at stage 2 (see above).

In case of player B:
If you act as player B, you do not make any decision in stage 1. Your score at the end of stage 2 is calculated as following:

$$\text{Score } \mathbf{B} = \mathbf{Z}_B$$

$\mathbf{Z}_B$ is a number that you select at stage 2. You can choose between $Z_B = 0$ and $\mathbf{Z}_B = \mathbf{1}$. The selected value will be taken into account for the calculation of your score. If you choose $Z_B = 0$, this costs you nothing. If you choose $\mathbf{Z}_B = \mathbf{1}$, this costs you $\mathbf{C}_B = \mathbf{24}$ Talers.
At the end of stage 2, the scores of both players are compared. The person with the **higher score** gets **100 Talers**. The other person gets **zero Talers**. If both persons have the same score, the higher one will be determined at random. In any case the costs of a chosen number will be subtracted from the already achieved Talers.

Course of a round
Stage 1:
First you get the following information:

- which of the roles A and B is assigned to you

- in case of acting as **player A**: Information about your own costs C_A which occur if you choose $Z_A = 1$ at stage 2 and about the costs C_B of the other player that occur if he chooses $Z_B = 1$ at stage 2.

- in case of acting as **player B**: Information about your own costs C_B which occur if you choose $Z_B = 1$ at stage 2 and about the costs C_A of the other player that occur if he chooses $Z_A = 1$ at stage 2.

If you act as **player A**, at stage 1 you will be asked which of the **alternatives 1 or 2** you want to choose. After you have selected one of the alternatives, stage 2 of the experiment begins.

Stage 2:

At stage 2, both players are **informed** about the chosen **alternative of player A**.

After that, you and the other player are asked what you think, which number Z the other one will choose. **If your guess is correct you will get 15 Talers, otherwise nothing.**

Then both players choose a **number Z**.

- in case of being **player A**, you can choose between $Z_A = 0$ and $Z_A = 1$. This influences your score. If you choose $Z_A = 1$, costs of C_A occur.

- in case of being **player B**, you can choose between $Z_B = 0$ and $Z_B = 1$. This influences your score. If you choose $Z_B = 1$, costs of C_B occur.

After that, you and the other player are informed about the decisions and the scores, x is randomly selected and the player with the higher score is announced. In addition, you get informed how many Talers you would earn if this round were selected later. Hence, you get the following information:

Your score:
Score of the other player:
The player with the higher score is player _ .
Your guess was correct/false.
Additionally, you would get _ Talers
Altogether, you would get _ Talers in this round.

Then the next round begins with the same procedure. Altogether you play five rounds. At the end of round five, it is randomly chosen which round will be paid out. Thereafter, a questionnaire appears on the screen which you are to answer.

Overview about the possible payments:

Payment for the player with the higher score:
100 Talers
- costs C_A or C_B respectively, if $Z = 1$ was chosen
+ 15 Talers for a correct guess
of the other player's choice of Z

Payment for the player with the lower score:
0 Talers
- costs C_A or C_B respectively, if $Z = 1$ was chosen
+ 15 Talers for a correct guess
of the other player's choice of Z

The payments will be added to your experiment account. In addition you are paid 2.50 Euro for participating in our experiment.

Now please answer the comprehension questions below. As soon as all participants have answered them correctly, the ten trial rounds will start.

Please stay on your seat at the end of the experiment until we invoke your cabin number. Bring this instruction and your cabin number to the front. Only then the payment for your score can begin.

Thanks a lot for participating and good luck!

Chapter 5

Management Changes, Career Concerns and Earnings Management[1]

5.1 Introduction

While the previous chapters deal with the active risk choice of agents, uncertainty is exogenously given in this part of the thesis. We investigate earnings management in conjunction with pre-announced managerial turnover in a career concerns model.

In this chapter we introduce a theoretical model where both the departing and the new manager care about their reputation concerning their ability. Like in the classical career concerns models (compare for instance Fama (1980) or Holmström (1999)) the ability of the managers is unknown for all participants. The market uses reported earnings to derive its assessment about the ability of the managers. Hence, the managers have an incentive to bias accounting data in order to pretend to have a high ability. Usually accounting data is used to create financial statements and reduce the information asymmetry between organizations and market participants. However, as this data also serves to reduce the uncertainty about the ability of the managers it is not always reliable because managers may have an incentive to bias the data.

Following Schipper (1989) we define earnings management as an intervention in the external reporting process to obtain some private profit. The literature offers ample evidence that earnings management activities are especially popular before and after management changes. If a management

---

[1]This chapter is based upon Nieken and Sliwka (2008).

change is pre-announced there exits the so called "horizon problem" (compare for example Ronen and Yaari (2008) page 93). It occurs if the departing manager tries to distort accounting data to maximize his own utility. For example, Butler and Newman (1989) and Dechow and Sloan (1991) show that departing CEOs tend to reduce discretionary expenditures such as Research & Development or advertising to increase reported earnings during their last year in office. Furthermore, the research of Davidson et al. (2007) reveals that large discretionary accruals occur in the year before CEO turnover. According to the data of Reitenga and Tearney (2003) earnings management is stronger if the departing CEO retains his or her seat on the board of directors after retirement. Additionally Brickley et al. (1999) find evidence that the likelihood for a manager to serve as a director on his own board or as an outside director on other boards is strongly and positively related to the performance while being a CEO. Hence, the departing CEOs are concerned about their performance if they plan to become a member of a board after their retirement.

The new manager might want to bias the reported earnings as well which is also referred to as the "big bath", "Rumpelstilzchen accounting" or "wiping the plate clean" (Walsh (1991)). All these expressions describe for instance profit reducing write-offs or income-decreasing discretionary accruals. For example, Walsh (1991) or Wells (2002) present evidence from Australian companies that new managers reduce reported earnings in the year of management change. Following management changes there are a greater frequencies of asset write-offs (Strong and Meyer (1987) or Elliot and Shaw (1988)), income reducing accounting method changes (Moore (1973)), income reducing accounting accruals (Pourciau (1993)), and divestitures of previous investments (Weisbach (1995)). Whereas the empirical evidence for earnings management is manifold, there are surprisingly few models analyzing earnings management surrounding management changes theoretically. The model presented in this thesis is a step to fill this gap in literature.

No model, we are aware of, analyzes the consequences of pre-announced managerial turnover on earnings management activities of the outgoing and incoming manager. Therefore, we develop a model to study earnings management activities before and after a pre-announced replacement of a manager. In this chapter we show that both, the departing and the new manager have an incentive to distort earnings if both care about their reputation and the external market updates its assessment of the managers ability based on reported earnings. The old manager brings earnings forward to the period he leaves and the new manager shifts cash flow away from his early time in office. We also study the effects of bonus payments based on reported earnings on these activities. We show that higher bonuses reduce the incentives to manipulate earnings for the new manager but aggravate the problem for the old manager.

The remainder of the chapter is organized as follows. In Section 5.2 we introduce the model and we analyze the possible Nash Equilibria for the old and the new manager in Section 5.3. Empirical evidence and testable implications are offered in Section 5.4. Section 5.5 concludes.

5.2 The Model

We consider the following simple model with 3 periods. In the first period an incumbent manager is in place. He leaves the organization after this period and this is known already in period 1. His successor works for the organization during the last 2 periods. Following the career concerns literature (Holmström (1982), resp. Holmström (1999), see also Dewatripont et al. (1999a) and Dewatripont et al. (1999b)), we assume that there is symmetric uncertainty about the ability of both managers. The abilities of the outgoing as well as the incoming managers are normally distributed. We denote the ability of the old manager with a_O and the ability of the new one with a_N. The prior distribution of the managers' abilities are

$$a_O \sim N\left(m_O, \sigma_O^2\right) \text{ and}$$
$$a_N \sim N\left(m_N, \sigma_N^2\right).$$

In each period a manager makes a set of decisions that affect the performance of the organization. The quality of the decisions made in period t depends upon the ability of the manager in place. A key assumption of the model is that the actual earnings in period t depend on the performance made by the management in the present period but also on the quality of the managerial decisions made in the past. Actual earnings are

$$\begin{aligned} c_1 &= \eta a_O + a_O + \varepsilon_1 \\ c_2 &= \eta a_O + a_N + \varepsilon_2 \\ c_3 &= \eta a_N + a_N + \varepsilon_3 \end{aligned}$$

such that η (with $0 \leq \eta \leq 1$) measures the importance of past decisions for present earnings. In a sense η measures to what extend earnings are a *lagging indicator* for managerial ability.

Each manager can observe the actual earnings when being in office and has some discretion in affecting reported earnings. Hence, both managers are able to manipulate earnings reported to the market to some extend. The old manager can shift amount Δ_O from period 1 to period 2 (or vice versa) and the new manager an amount Δ_N between period 2 and period 3. This can for instance be done by influencing accruals. We impose a clean surplus accounting condition, that is if reported earnings are reduced (increased) by a certain amount relative to actual earnings in one period, they must be increased (reduced) by the same amount in a later period. The reported earnings are therefore characterized as:

$$
\begin{aligned}
r_1 &= c_1 - \Delta_O \\
r_2 &= c_2 + \Delta_O - \Delta_N \\
r_3 &= c_3 + \Delta_N
\end{aligned}
$$

However, shifting causes private manipulation costs for the manager like costs of deception or litigation which we denote with $\kappa(\Delta)$ where $\kappa'(\Delta) > 0$ and $\kappa''(\Delta) > 0$. For simplicity we assume that $\kappa(\Delta) = \frac{\kappa}{2}\Delta^2$.

We assume that each period the manager in place receives a bonus which is linear in reported earnings, i.e. equal to $\beta \cdot r_t$ with $0 \leq \beta \leq 1$. Yet, we also assume that managers are also interested in their reputation. Here, this reputational utility is determined by the market's beliefs about their respective ability at the end of their last period in office. The outgoing and incoming managers' reputational utilities are given by

$$
\begin{aligned}
u_O^R &= E_M[a_O | r_1] \cdot U_O^R \text{ and} \\
u_N^R &= E_M[a_N | r_1, r_2, r_3] \cdot U_N^R
\end{aligned}
$$

where $E_M[a_O | r_1]$ resp. $E_M[a_N | r_1, r_2, r_3]$ is the expected ability of the manager the market has estimated based on the observation of the reported earnings and on the manager's equilibrium strategy. U_O^R and U_N^R measure the importance of a manager's reputation for his or her utility. The idea is that managers care for their public image and therefore receive some utility depending on the expected ability when viewed by some outside observer. The external reputation is important as it determines, for instance, the number of external board memberships, the manager's social status or his coverage in the business press.

Finally, we assume that both managers discount future income and reputational utility with a discount factor δ.

As the outgoing manager has been in office earlier on there should be less uncertainty about his ability. Therefore we should usually expect that $\sigma_O^2 < \sigma_N^2$. Furthermore, although retiring managers will also care for their reputation, we should typically expect reputational concerns to have a stronger effect on the incoming manager's utility such that $U_N^R > U_O^R$.

5.3 Equilibrium Analysis

We now investigate Perfect Bayesian Equilibria of the game described above. The old manager only cares about his reputation after period 1. The utility function of the old manager in period 1 is therefore:

$$\beta \cdot r_1 + E\left[E_M\left[a_O \mid r_1\right] \cdot U_O^R\right] - \frac{\kappa}{2}\Delta_O^2.$$

It is important to note that the market rationally anticipates the manager's incentives to manipulate reported earnings. We start by assuming that the manager follows a linear shifting strategy. Given that the market believes the manager follows such a linear strategy, we will show that the manager's best response is indeed linear. We then determine values for the slope and the intercept of the linear strategy such that the market's beliefs are consistent with the manager's best response thereby establishing the existence of a Perfect Bayesian Equilibrium.

As the old manager can privately observe c_1 a linear shifting strategy is given by

$$\Delta_O\left(c_1\right) = \gamma_{1O} + \gamma_{2O} \cdot c_1.$$

Since actual earnings are normally distributed, reported earnings will be normally distributed as well. Based on the market's prior expectations on the manager's ability, the observed report r_1, and the supposed shifting strategy, the market updates its beliefs on the manager's talent. As $c_1 - \gamma_{1O} - \gamma_{2O} \cdot c_1$ is normally distributed, we can conclude that[2]

$$
\begin{aligned}
E_M\left[a_O \mid r_1\right] &= m_O + \frac{Cov[a_O,(1-\gamma_{2O})((\eta+1)a_O+\varepsilon_1)-\gamma_{1O}]}{Var[(1-\gamma_{2O})((\eta+1)a_O+\varepsilon_1)-\gamma_{1O}]} \\
&\quad \cdot (r_1 - E\left[(1 - \gamma_{2O})\left((\eta + 1)a_O + \varepsilon_1\right) - \gamma_{1O}\right]) \\
&= m_O + \frac{(\eta+1)\sigma_O^2(r_1-((1-\gamma_{2O})(\eta+1)m_O-\gamma_{1O}))}{(1-\gamma_{2O})\left((\eta+1)^2\sigma_O^2+\sigma_\varepsilon^2\right)}.
\end{aligned}
$$

Hence, the old manager chooses the optimal amount of shifted earnings Δ_O by maximizing

$$
\max_{\Delta_O} \quad \beta \cdot r_1 + \left(m_O + \frac{(\eta+1)\sigma_O^2(r_1-((1-\gamma_{2O})(\eta+1)m_O-\gamma_{1O}))}{(1-\gamma_{2O})\left((\eta+1)^2\sigma_O^2+\sigma_\varepsilon^2\right)}\right) \cdot U_O^R - \frac{\kappa}{2}\Delta_O^2.
$$

$$\text{s.t.} \quad r_1 = c_1 - \Delta_O$$

---

[2] We use that $E\left[Y \mid X\right] = E\left[Y\right] + \frac{Cov[X,Y]}{Var[X]}\left(X - E\left[X\right]\right)$ if X and Y are normally distributed random variables (compare for instance Gourieroux and Monfort (1989) page 524.)

From solving this maximization problem, we obtain the manager's best response function. In equilibrium, this best response function must correspond to the market's beliefs about the manager's shifting strategy. Solving for this equilibrium strategy we obtain the following result.

Proposition 1 *A Perfect Bayesian Equilibrium exists in which the old manager shifts*

$$\Delta_O^* = -\frac{1}{\kappa}\left(\beta + \frac{(\eta+1)\,\sigma_O^2}{(\eta+1)^2\,\sigma_O^2 + \sigma_\varepsilon^2}\cdot U_O^R\right)$$

such that he increases reported earnings in period 1 at the expense of future earnings. The old manager will manipulate earnings to a stronger degree, if his bonus depends to a stronger extent on reported earnings (high β), he cares more for his reputation (high U_O^R) and there is more prior uncertainty on his ability (high σ_O^2). He manipulates less if earnings are more volatile (high σ_ε^2) and the costs of manipulation (high κ) are higher.

Proof: See Appendix.

The old manager brings a certain amount forward from period 2 to increase the reported earnings in period 1. The amount the old manager shifts depends on the size of the bonus payment, the variance of the noise term, the variance of his own ability and the shifting costs. It is straightforward to understand that higher values of the bonus slope β lead to more forward shifting by the outgoing manager as he only benefits from earnings in the first period and no longer from second period earnings.

Yet, this is not the only reason to shift earnings to the first period as he also takes reputational concerns into account. If the variance of the noise term is higher the amount shifted is lower because reported earnings are then a less valid indicator for the manager's ability. However, the higher the remaining uncertainty on the old manager's ability σ_O^2, the stronger is the effect of the reported earnings on his reputation and in turn the stronger are the manager's incentives to manipulate earnings in his last year in office.

Still, as laid out above, we would expect that there is not so much uncertainty about the ability of an incumbent manager and hence, σ_O^2 should typically be rather low. Furthermore, we should expect much higher uncertainty about a newly hired manager's ability. Hence, it is interesting to investigate the incentives for earnings management of the new manager in the later periods.

The new manager also cares about his reputation after his last period in office, which is period 3. The market again anticipates that the new manager can also manipulate reported earnings. As before, we first assume the market to suppose that the new manager follows a linear manipulation strategy

$$\Delta_N(c_1, c_2) = \gamma_N + \gamma_{1N} c_1 + \gamma_{2N} c_2.$$

It is important to note that the market's assessment now may depend on the reported earnings in all periods 1, 2, and 3. As all these earnings are normally distributed random variables the market's assessment after period 3 is[3]

$$
\begin{aligned}
& E_M\left[a_N \mid r_1, r_2, r_3\right] \\
& = m_N + \begin{pmatrix} \sigma_{r_1 a_N} & \sigma_{r_2 a_N} & \sigma_{r_3 a_N} \end{pmatrix} \cdot \underbrace{\begin{pmatrix} \sigma_{r_1}^2 & \sigma_{r_1 r_2} & \sigma_{r_1 r_3} \\ \sigma_{r_1 r_2} & \sigma_{r_2}^2 & \sigma_{r_2 r_3} \\ \sigma_{r_1 r_3} & \sigma_{r_2 r_3} & \sigma_{r_3}^2 \end{pmatrix}^{-1}}_{=\Sigma} \cdot \begin{pmatrix} r_1 - E[r_1] \\ r_2 - E[r_2] \\ r_3 - E[r_3] \end{pmatrix}
\end{aligned}
$$

where $\sigma_{r_t a_N}$ denotes the covariance between r_t and a_N.

The new manager maximizes his expected utility in period 2

$$\max_{\Delta_N} \quad \beta(r_2 + \delta r_3) + \delta \cdot E\left[E_M\left[a_N \mid r_1, r_2, r_3\right] \mid c_1, c_2\right] \cdot U_N^R - \frac{\kappa}{2} \Delta_N^2.$$

$$\text{s.t.} \quad r_2 = c_2 + \Delta_O - \Delta_N$$

$$r_3 = c_3 + \Delta_N$$

By solving this optimization problem and then seeking for beliefs consistent with the equilibrium strategies, we obtain the following result.

Proposition 2 *A Perfect Bayesian Equilibrium exists in which the new manager shifts earnings*

$$\Delta_N^* = -\frac{\beta}{\kappa}(1-\delta) + \delta \cdot \frac{U_N^R}{\kappa} \cdot \eta \frac{(1+2\eta^2+3\eta)\sigma_O^2 + \sigma_\varepsilon^2}{\left(\frac{\sigma_\varepsilon^2}{\sigma_N^2} + (1+2\eta+2\eta^2)\frac{\sigma_O^2}{\sigma_N^2} + 2 + 2\eta + \eta^2\right)\sigma_\varepsilon^2 + (2+6\eta+8\eta^2+6\eta^3+2\eta^4)\sigma_O^2}$$

from period 2 to 3. The new manager shifts a larger amount if he cares more for his reputation (high U_N^R), there is more prior uncertainty on his ability (high σ_N^2), and if there is more uncertainty about the ability of the old manager (high σ_O^2). He manipulates less when earnings are more volatile (high σ_ε^2) and the costs of manipulation (high κ) are higher.

Proof: See Appendix.

---

[3]See again Gourieroux and Monfort (1989) page 524 for the proof that $E[Y|X] = E[Y] + \frac{Cov[X,Y]}{Var[X]}(X - E[X])$ also holds for vectors of random variables.

The new manager also has an incentive to shift earnings to influence his variable compensation as well as his reputation. Yet, in contrast to the outgoing manager there is a trade-off between both reasons for shifting. On the one hand, as the manager discounts future income he has an incentive to increase present earnings at the expense of future earnings. But reputational concerns create an incentive to shift earnings backwards from period 2 to period 3. Note that this is the case although reported earnings in period 2 already affect his reputation. The reason is that his ability has a stronger effect on earnings in period 3 than on those in period 2 as second period earnings are not only affected by his own decisions but also by the decisions made by his predecessor in the past and therefore will still be attributed to some extend to the performance of his predecessor. This causes an incentive to reduce second period profits to increase those in the third period. These reputational incentives to manipulate earnings are of course stronger, the more the manager cares for his reputation (the higher U_N^R) the lower the earnings volatility σ_ε^2 and the higher the values of the prior variance of his ability σ_N^2.

It is interesting to note that the *new* manager's incentives to shift earnings to the future are stronger the higher the uncertainty on the *old* manager's ability σ_O^2. To understand this effect consider the following: If σ_O^2 is large, there is still a high uncertainty on the old manager's ability and in turn, variations in second period outcomes cannot be attributed precisely to the relative contributions of the old and the new manager. In this case the second period outcome is only a weak signal of the new manager's ability and will therefore have a weak impact on his reputation. As the third period outcome is a much stronger signal about his ability and it has a larger impact on his reputation there are strong incentives to shift cash flow to the third period in this case. If, however, the ability of the old manager is very well known (σ_O^2 is small) the second period result is already a more precise signal on the new manager's ability. Hence, there are weaker incentives to shift cash flow to later periods in this case.

5.4 Empirical Evidence and Testable Implications

In this section we discuss various testable implications which can be derived from our model. We start with research questions concerning the uncertainty about the ability of the old manager. The shorter the previous career and especially the tenure at the current position, the higher will the uncertainty about the ability of the old manager be. Hence, we expect the amount of cash flow shifted by both the outgoing and the new manager to be higher if the tenure of the outgoing manager is shorter. A similar reasoning applies regarding the career of the new manager. If the previous career of the new manager is short or if he has been employed in a different industry the market will initially not have very precise information about his ability. In contrast if he has worked in a similar industry or even in the same organization the uncertainty about his ability will be lower.[4] Therefore, we expect new managers to shift more if they are younger or if they have previously been employed in a different industry.

We furthermore expect lower levels of earnings management in highly volatile industries or economic conditions compared to organizations operating in a relatively stable environment. A higher volatility causes greater noise and reduces the information contained in reported earnings on the manager's abilities.

A rather straightforward prediction of the model is that the incentives for both managers to manage earnings are lower if the shifting costs are high. The shifting costs are for example higher if the auditing quality and therefore the probability of being detected is higher. For instance, if the organization is a client of one of the Big Four auditors earnings management should be lower. Compare for example Becker et al. (1998) who investigate the impact of auditing quality on earnings management. They show that the discretionary accruals are higher if a company is not a client of one of the Big Six auditors in the United States. Another factor influencing shifting costs are the accounting standards. If the accounting standards offer very easy ways to manipulate reported earnings we expect both managers to shift a higher amount of money. When comparing different accounting standards or changes in accounting rules one should find more shifting if the rules are less strict.

It is also very interesting to investigate the interplay of compensation and earnings management surrounding management changes. Following the predictions of our model we expect the old manager to shift more to his last periods in office if his bonus depends to a stronger extend on reported earnings. Hence, higher bonus payment leads to a stronger "horizon problem". Davidson et al. (2007) provide evidence that CEOs near retirement shift money to the years prior to their turnover.

Finally, it is interesting to discuss how the outgoing manager's incentives

---

[4]In particular, this should be the case if the new manager has for instance been the head of a division within the same company with full responsibility for profits and losses.

to manipulate earnings are affected by potential hopes to retain a board seat after retirement. On the one hand, such plans may lead to a longer term orientation and hence to lower earnings management activities in the last period in office. This can be shown in a very simple extension of our model: If the outgoing manager receives a bonus also in period 2 after his retirement depending on r_2 he shifts lower amounts in period 1.[5] Yet, on the other hand, the financial results at the end of his time in office could be decisive for the opportunity to retain a board seat. In this case such considerations should lead to stronger reputational concerns and, hence, more earnings management activities. Reitenga and Tearney (2003) for instance show that departing CEOs exert more earnings management if they retain a board seat after retirement.

5.5 Conclusion

We have investigated the effects of management turnover on earnings management in a principal agent model. In our setup there is an old manager who leaves after the first period and a new manager who is in place in period 2 and 3. The ability of both managers is unknown and the market updates its assessment of the ability after observing the reported earnings. We show that both managers bias the reported earnings to influence the belief of the market. Reputational concerns cause incentives for the outgoing manager to shift earnings forward but for a new manager to shift earnings backward to later periods in office. The level of the bias depends on several parameters. High cost of manipulating or a high variance of the noise term decrease the amount shifted by both the outgoing and the new manager. More uncertainty about the managers' ability leads to more earnings management activities by the old as well as the new manager. Finally, we have shown that whereas bonus payments aggravate the incentives for earnings management for the outgoing manager, they mitigate those incentives for new managers.

Of course, there are still many open questions for future research. We have derived several predictions that can be tested empirically. Furthermore, we so far do not consider investment decisions in our model. It would, for instance, be interesting to study the effects of reputational concerns on the interplay of investment decisions and earnings management in a formal model.

---

[5] An alternative interpretation for such an extension would be that the outgoing manager holds stock options after retirment and the stock price is affected by second period reported earnings.

5.6 Appendix to Chapter 5

Proof of Proposition 1:

The first order condition of the old manager's optimization problem is

$$-\beta - \frac{(\eta + 1)\,\sigma_O^2}{(1 - \gamma_{2O})\left((\eta + 1)^2\,\sigma_O^2 + \sigma_\varepsilon^2\right)} \cdot U_O^R - \kappa\Delta_O \overset{!}{=} 0.$$

$$\Leftrightarrow \Delta_O = -\frac{1}{\kappa}\left(\beta + \frac{(\eta + 1)\,\sigma_O^2}{(1 - \gamma_{2O})\left((\eta + 1)^2\,\sigma_O^2 + \sigma_\varepsilon^2\right)} \cdot U_O^R\right)$$

In a Perfect Bayesian Equilibrium, the market's beliefs must be consistent with the manager's strategy, hence

$$-\frac{1}{\kappa}\left(\beta + \frac{(\eta + 1)\,\sigma_O^2}{(1 - \gamma_{2O})\left((\eta + 1)^2\,\sigma_O^2 + \sigma_\varepsilon^2\right)} \cdot U_O^R\right) = \gamma_{1O} + \gamma_{2O}c_1,$$

and we must have that

$$\Leftrightarrow \quad \gamma_{1O}^* = -\frac{1}{\kappa}\left(\beta + \frac{(\eta + 1)\,\sigma_O^2 \cdot U_O^R}{(\eta + 1)^2\,\sigma_O^2 + \sigma_\varepsilon^2}\right) \quad \text{and}$$

$$\Leftrightarrow \quad \gamma_{2O}^* = 0.$$

■

Proof of Proposition 2:

First, consider the market's assessment of the new manager's ability. Note that $\sigma_{r_1 a_N} = 0$ and hence,

$$E_M\left[a_N \,|\, r_1, r_2, r_3\right] \tag{5.1}$$
$$= m_N + (r_3 - E\left[r_3\right])$$
$$\left(\frac{\sigma_{r_2 a_N}\left(\sigma_{r_1}^2\sigma_{r_2 r_3} - \sigma_{r_1 r_2}\sigma_{r_1 r_3}\right) + \sigma_{r_3 a_N}\left(\sigma_{r_1 r_2}^2 - \sigma_{r_1}^2\sigma_{r_2}^2\right)}{\sigma_{r_1}^2\sigma_{r_2 r_3}^2 + \sigma_{r_3}^2\sigma_{r_1 r_2}^2 - \sigma_{r_1}^2\sigma_{r_2}^2\sigma_{r_3}^2 - 2\sigma_{r_1 r_2}\sigma_{r_1 r_3}\sigma_{r_2 r_3} + \sigma_{r_2}^2\sigma_{r_1 r_3}^2}\right)$$
$$+ (r_2 - E\left[r_2\right])$$
$$\left(\frac{\sigma_{r_2 a_N}\left(\sigma_{r_1 r_3}^2 -\right) + \sigma_{r_3 a_N}\left(\sigma_{r_1}^2\sigma_{r_2 r_3} - \sigma_{r_1 r_2}\sigma_{r_1 r_3}\right)}{\sigma_{r_1}^2\sigma_{r_2 r_3}^2 + \sigma_{r_3}^2\sigma_{r_1 r_2}^2 - \sigma_{r_1}^2\sigma_{r_2}^2\sigma_{r_3}^2 - 2\sigma_{r_1 r_2}\sigma_{r_1 r_3}\sigma_{r_2 r_3} + \sigma_{r_2}^2\sigma_{r_1 r_3}^2}\right)$$
$$+ (r_1 - E\left[r_1\right])$$
$$\left(\frac{\sigma_{r_2 a_N}\left(\sigma_{r_3}^2\sigma_{r_1 r_2} - \sigma_{r_2 r_3}\sigma_{r_1 r_3}\right) + \sigma_{r_3 a_N}\left(\sigma_{r_2}^2\sigma_{r_1 r_3} - \sigma_{r_1 r_2}\sigma_{r_2 r_3}\right)}{\sigma_{r_1}^2\sigma_{r_2 r_3}^2 + \sigma_{r_3}^2\sigma_{r_1 r_2}^2 - \sigma_{r_1}^2\sigma_{r_2}^2\sigma_{r_3}^2 - 2\sigma_{r_1 r_2}\sigma_{r_1 r_3}\sigma_{r_2 r_3} + \sigma_{r_2}^2\sigma_{r_1 r_3}^2}\right).$$

The new manager maximizes

$$\max_{\Delta_N} \quad \beta\left(r_2 + \delta r_3\right) + \delta \cdot E\left[E_M\left[a_N \,|\, r_1, r_2, r_3\right]\big|\, c_1, c_2\right] \cdot U_N^R - \frac{\kappa}{2}\Delta_N^2$$
$$\text{s.t. } r_2 = c_2 + \Delta_O - \Delta_N$$
$$r_3 = c_3 + \Delta_N$$

or

$$\max_{\Delta_N} \quad \beta\left(c_2 + \Delta_O - \Delta_N + \delta\left(c_3 + \Delta_N\right)\right) + \delta \cdot E\left[E_M\left[a_N \,|\, r_1, r_2, r_3\right]\big|\, c_1, c_2\right] \cdot U_N^R - \frac{\kappa}{2}\Delta_N^2.$$

Using (5.1) we obtain the following first-order condition

$$\delta \cdot U_N^R \left(\frac{\sigma_{r_2 a_N}\left(\sigma_{r_1}^2\sigma_{r_2 r_3} + \sigma_{r_1}^2\sigma_{r_3}^2 - \sigma_{r_1 r_2}\sigma_{r_1 r_3} - \sigma_{r_1 r_3}^2\right)}{\sigma_{r_1}^2\left(\sigma_{r_2 r_3}^2 - \sigma_{r_2}^2\sigma_{r_3}^2\right) + \sigma_{r_3}^2\sigma_{r_1 r_2}^2 + \sigma_{r_1 r_3}\left(\sigma_{r_2}^2\sigma_{r_1 r_3} - 2\sigma_{r_1 r_2}\sigma_{r_2 r_3}\right)}\right.$$
$$\left. - \frac{\sigma_{r_3 a_N}\left(\sigma_{r_1}^2\sigma_{r_2}^2 + \sigma_{r_1}^2\sigma_{r_2 r_3} - \sigma_{r_1 r_2}^2 - \sigma_{r_1 r_2}\sigma_{r_1 r_3}\right)}{\sigma_{r_1}^2\left(\sigma_{r_2 r_3}^2 - \sigma_{r_2}^2\sigma_{r_3}^2\right) + \sigma_{r_3}^2\sigma_{r_1 r_2}^2 + \sigma_{r_1 r_3}\left(\sigma_{r_2}^2\sigma_{r_1 r_3} - 2\sigma_{r_1 r_2}\sigma_{r_2 r_3}\right)}\right)$$
$$- \beta\left(1 - \delta\right) - \kappa\Delta_N \overset{!}{=} 0.$$

In equilibrium we must therefore have

$$\gamma_N + \gamma_{1N} c_1 + \gamma_{2N} c_2 \tag{5.2}$$

$$= -\frac{\beta}{\kappa} (1 - \delta)$$

$$+ \delta \cdot U_N^R \left(\frac{\sigma_{r_2 a_N} \left(\sigma_{r_1}^2 \sigma_{r_2 r_3} + \sigma_{r_1}^2 \sigma_{r_3}^2 - \sigma_{r_1 r_2} \sigma_{r_1 r_3} - \sigma_{r_1 r_3}^2 \right)}{\sigma_{r_1}^2 \left(\sigma_{r_2 r_3}^2 - \sigma_{r_2}^2 \sigma_{r_3}^2 \right) + \sigma_{r_3}^2 \sigma_{r_1 r_2}^2 + \sigma_{r_1 r_3} \left(\sigma_{r_2}^2 \sigma_{r_1 r_3} - 2\sigma_{r_1 r_2} \sigma_{r_2 r_3} \right)} \right.$$

$$\left. - \frac{\sigma_{r_3 a_N} \left(\sigma_{r_1}^2 \sigma_{r_2}^2 + \sigma_{r_1}^2 \sigma_{r_2 r_3} - \sigma_{r_1 r_2}^2 - \sigma_{r_1 r_2} \sigma_{r_1 r_3} \right)}{\sigma_{r_1}^2 \left(\sigma_{r_2 r_3}^2 - \sigma_{r_2}^2 \sigma_{r_3}^2 \right) + \sigma_{r_3}^2 \sigma_{r_1 r_2}^2 + \sigma_{r_1 r_3} \left(\sigma_{r_2}^2 \sigma_{r_1 r_3} - 2\sigma_{r_1 r_2} \sigma_{r_2 r_3} \right)} \right).$$

The variance and covariance terms in this expression are:

$$\sigma_{r_1}^2 = \left((1 - \gamma_{2O})(\eta + 1) \right)^2 \sigma_O^2 + (1 - \gamma_{2O})^2 \sigma_\varepsilon^2$$

$$\sigma_{r_2}^2 = \left((1 - \gamma_{2N}) \eta + (\gamma_{2O} - \gamma_{1N})(\eta + 1) \right)^2 \sigma_O^2 + (1 - \gamma_{2N})^2 \sigma_N^2$$
$$\quad + \left((1 - \gamma_{2N})^2 + (\gamma_{2O} - \gamma_{1N})^2 \right) \sigma_\varepsilon^2$$

$$\sigma_{r_3}^2 = (\eta + 1 + \gamma_{2N})^2 \sigma_N^2 + (\gamma_{1N}(1 + \eta) + \gamma_{2N}\eta)^2 \sigma_O^2 + (\gamma_{1N}^2 + \gamma_{2N}^2 + 1) \sigma_\varepsilon^2$$

$$\sigma_{r_1 r_2} = (1 - \gamma_{2O})(\eta + 1) \left((1 - \gamma_{2N}) \eta + (\gamma_{2O} - \gamma_{1N})(\eta + 1) \right) \sigma_O^2$$
$$\quad + (1 - \gamma_{2O})(\gamma_{2O} - \gamma_{1N}) \sigma_\varepsilon^2$$

$$\sigma_{r_2 r_3} = \left((1 - \gamma_{2N}) \eta + (\gamma_{2O} - \gamma_{1N})(\eta + 1) \right) \left(\gamma_{1N}(1 + \eta) + \gamma_{2N}\eta \right) \sigma_O^2$$
$$\quad + (1 - \gamma_{2N})(\eta + 1 + \gamma_{2N}) \sigma_N^2 + \left((1 - \gamma_{2N}) \gamma_{2N} + (\gamma_{2O} - \gamma_{1N}) \gamma_{1N} \right) \sigma_\varepsilon^2$$

$$\sigma_{r_1 r_3} = (1 - \gamma_{2O})(\eta + 1) \left(\gamma_{1N}(1 + \eta) + \gamma_{2N}\eta \right) \sigma_O^2 + (1 - \gamma_{2O}) \gamma_{1N} \sigma_\varepsilon^2$$

$$\sigma_{r_2 a_N} = (1 - \gamma_{2N}) \sigma_N^2$$

$$\sigma_{r_3 a_N} = (\eta + 1 + \gamma_{2N}) \sigma_N^2$$

As the right hand side of (5.2) does not depend on c_1 and c_2, γ_{1N} and γ_{2N} have to be zero in equilibrium. Furthermore because of Proposition 1 we know that also $\gamma_{2O} = 0$. Inserting these expressions in (5.2) and simplifying yields

$$\Delta_N = \gamma_N = -\frac{\beta}{\kappa} (1 - \delta) + \delta \cdot \frac{U_N^R}{\kappa} \eta \frac{(1 + 2\eta^2 + 3\eta) \sigma_O^2 + \sigma_\varepsilon^2}{\left(\frac{\sigma_\varepsilon^2}{\sigma_N^2} + (1 + 2\eta + 2\eta^2) \frac{\sigma_O^2}{\sigma_N^2} + 2 + 2\eta + \eta^2 \right) \sigma_\varepsilon^2 + (2 + 6\eta + 8\eta^2 + 6\eta^3 + 2\eta^4) \sigma_O^2}.$$

Note that this expression is increasing in σ_N^2. Furthermore, the first derivative of this expression with respect to σ_O^2 is positive if and only if

$$2\sigma_N^2 + 3\eta \sigma_N^2 + \eta^2 \sigma_N^2 + \sigma_\varepsilon^2 > 0$$

which is always the case. The first derivative with respect to σ_ε^2 is negative if and only if

$$- \left(\eta^2 + 3\eta + 2\right) \eta \sigma_N^2 - \left(4\eta^4 + 10\eta^3 10\eta^2 + 5\eta + 1\right) \sigma_O^2 - \left(4\eta^2 + 6\eta + 2\right) \sigma_\varepsilon^2 - \frac{\sigma_\varepsilon^4}{\sigma_O^2} < 0$$

which also always holds. ∎

Bibliography

Amegashie, J. A. (2007): American Idol: Should it be a Singing Contest or a Popularity Contest? CESifo Working Paper Series: No. 2171.

Baker, G. P., Gibbs, M. and Holmström, B. (1994): The Wage Policy of a Firm. Quarterly Journal of Economics, 109, pp. 921–955.

Baker, T., Collins, D. and Reitenga, A. L. (2003): Stock Option Compensation and Earnings Management. Journal of Accounting, Auditing & Finance, 18, pp. 557–582.

Becker, B. E. and Huselid, M. A. (1992): The Incentive Effects of Tournament Compensation Systems. Administrative Science Quarterly, 37, pp. 336–350.

Becker, C. L., DeFond, M. L., Jiambavlo, J. and Subramanyam, K. R. (1998): The Effect of Audit Quality on Earnings Management. Contemporary Accounting Research, 15, pp. 1–24.

Beneish, M. D. (2001): Earnings Management: A Perspective. Managerial Finance, 27, pp. 3–17.

Bergstresser, D. and Philippon, T. (2006): CEO Incentives and Earnings Management. Journal of Financial Economics, 80, pp. 511–529.

Binmore, K., McCarthy, J., Ponti, G., Samuelson, L. and Shaked, A. (2002): A Backward Induction Experiment. Journal of Economic Theory, 104, pp. 48–88.

Bothner, M. S., Kang, J. and Stuart, T. E. (2007): Competitive Crowding and Risk Taking in a Tournament: Evidence from NASCAR Racing. Administrative Science Quarterly, 52, pp. 208–247.

Brickley, J. A., Linck, J. S. and Coles, J. L. (1999): What Happens to CEOs after They Retire? New Evidence on Career Concerns, Horizon Problems, and CEO Incentives. Journal of Financial Economics, 52, pp. 341–377.

Brown, K. C., Harlow, W. V. and Starks, L. T. (1996): Of Tournaments and Temptations: An Analysis of Managerial Incentives in the Mutual Fund Industry. Journal of Finance, 51, pp. 85–110.

Bull, C., Schotter, A. and Weigelt, K. (1987): Tournaments and Piece Rates: An Experimental Study. Journal of Political Economy, 95, pp. 1–33.

Busse, J. A. (2001): Another Look at Mutual Fund Tournaments. Journal of Financial and Quantitative Analysis, 36, pp. 53–73.

Butler, S. and Newman, H. (1989): Agency Control Mechanisms, Effectiveness and Decision Making in an Executive's Final Year with the Firm. Journal of Institutional and Theoretical Economics, 145, pp. 451–464.

Camerer, C. (2003): Behavioral Game Theory: Experiments on Strategic Interaction. Princeton University Press, Princeton.

Caplin, A. S. and Nalebuff, B. J. (1986): Multi-dimensional Product Differentiation and Price Competition. Oxford Economic Papers, 38, pp. 129–145.

Chevalier, J. A. and Ellison, G. D. (1997): Risk Taking by Mutual Funds as a Response to Incentives. Journal of Political Economy, 105, pp. 1167–1200.

Clark, D. J. and Riis, C. (1998): Competition over More Than One Prize. American Economic Review, 88, pp. 276–289.

Dannenberg, A., Riechmann, T., Sturm, B. and Vogt, C. (2007): Inequity Aversion and Individual Behavior in Public Good Games: An Experimental Investigation. ZEW Discussion Paper No. 07-034.

Davidson, W. N., Xie, B., Xu, W. and Ning, Y. (2007): The influence of executive age, career horizon and incentives on pre-turnover earnings management. Journal of Management and Governance, 11, pp. 45–60.

Dechow, P. M. and Skinner, D. J. (2000): Earnings Management: Views of Account Academics, Practitioners, and Regulators. Accounting Horizons, 14, pp. 235–250.

Dechow, P. M. and Sloan, R. G. (1991): Executive Incentives and the Horizon Problem. Journal of Accounting and Economics, 14, pp. 51–89.

DeFond, M. L. and Park, C. W. (1997): Smoothing income in anticipation of future earnings. Journal of Accounting and Economics, 23, pp. 115–139.

DeVaro, J. (2006): Internal promotion competitions in firms. RAND Journal of Economics, 37, pp. 521–542.

Dewatripont, M., Jewitt, I. and Tirole, J. (1999a): The Economics of Career Concerns, Part I: Comparing Information Structures. Review of Economic Studies, 66, pp. 183–198.

Dewatripont, M., Jewitt, I. and Tirole, J. (1999b): The Economics of Career Concerns, Part II: Application to Missions and Accountability of Government Agencies. Review of Economic Studies, 66, pp. 199–207.

Dohmen, T., Falk, A., Huffman, D., Sunde, U., Schupp, J. and Wagner, G. G. (2005): Individual Risk Attitudes: New Evidence from a Large, Representative, Experimentally-Validated Survey. IZA Discussion Paper No. 1730.

Ehrenberg, R. G. and Bognanno, M. L. (1990): Do Tournaments Have Incentive Effects? Journal of Political Economy, 98, pp. 1307–1324.

Elliot, J.A. and Shaw, W. H. (1988): Write-offs as Accounting Procedures to Manage Perceptions. Journal of Accounting Research (supplement), 26, pp. 91–119.

Eriksson, T. (1999): Executive Compensation and Tournament Theory: Empirical Tests on Danish Data. Journal of Labor Economics, 17, pp. 262–280.

Fama, E. (1980): Agency Problems and the Theory of the Firm. Journal of Political Economy, 88, pp. 288–307.

Fehr, E. and Schmidt, K. M. (1999): A Theory of Fairness, Competition, and Cooperation. Quarterly Journal of Economics, 114, pp. 817–868.

Fernie, S. and Metcalf, D. (1999): It's Not What You Pay It's the Way that You Pay It and that's What Gets Results: Jockey's Pay and Performance. Labour, 13, pp. 385–411.

Fischbacher, U. (2007): z-Tree - Zurich Toolbox for Readymade Economic Experiments. Experimental Economics, 10, pp. 171–178.

Fudenberg, D. and Tirole, J. (1995): A Theory of Income and Dividend Smoothing Based on Incumbency Rents. Journal of Political Economy, 103, pp. 75–93.

Gaba, A. and Kalra, A. (1999): Risk Behavior in Response to Quotas and Contests. Marketing Science, 18, pp. 417–434.

Garvey, G. and Milbourn, T. (2003): Incentive Compensation When Executives Can Hedge the Market: Evidence of Relative Performance Evaluation in the Cross Section. Journal of Finance, 58, pp. 1557–1582.

Geradin, D. (2006): The liberalization of network industries in the European Union: where do we come from and where do we go? Prime Minister's Office, Economic Council of Finland.

Goeree, J. K and Holt, C. A. (2001): Ten Little Treasures of Game Theory and Ten Intuitive Contradictions. American Economic Review, 91, pp. 1402–1422.

Gourieroux, C. and Monfort, A. (1989): Statistique et Modèles Économétriques, Vol. 2. Economica, Paris.

Green, J. R. and Stokey, N. L. (1983): A Comparison of Tournaments and Contracts. Journal of Political Economy, 91, pp. 349–364.

Greiner, B. (2003): An Online Recruitment System for Economic Experiments. In: Kremer, K. and Macho, V. (Ed.) Forschung und wissenschaftliches Rechnen, GWDG Bericht 63, Göttingen: Gesellschaft für Wissenschaftliche Datenverarbeitung, pp. 79–93.

Grund, C. and Sliwka, D. (2005): Envy and Compassion in Tournaments. Journal of Economics and Management Strategy, 14, pp. 187–207.

Guidry, F., Leone, A. J. and Rock, S. (1999): Earnings-based bonus plans and earnings management by business-unit managers. Journal of Accounting and Economics, 26, pp. 113–142.

Harbring, C. and Irlenbusch, B. (2003): An experimental study on tournament design. Labour Economics, 10, pp. 443–464.

Harbring, C., Irlenbusch, B., Kräkel, M. and Selten, R. (2007): Sabotage in corporate contests - an experimental analysis. International Journal of the Economics of Business, 14, pp. 367–392.

Healy, P. M. (1985): The Effect of Bonus Schemes on Accounting Decisions. Journal of Accounting and Economics, 7, pp. 85–107.

Healy, P. M. and Wahlen, J. M. (1999): A Review of the Earnings Management Literature and Its Implications for Standard Setting. Accounting Horizons, 13, pp. 365–389.

Ho, T., Camerer, C. and Weigelt, K. (1998): Iterated Dominance and Iterated Best Response in Experimental p-Beauty-Contests. American Economic Review, 88, pp. 947–969.

Holmström, B. (1982): Managerial Incentive Problems - A Dynamic Perspective. In: Essays in Economics and Management in Honor of Lars Wahlbeck, Helsinki.

Holmström, B. (1999): Managerial Incentive Problems: A Dynamic Perspective. Review of Economic Studies, 66, pp. 169–182.

Hvide, H. K. (2002): Tournament Rewards and Risk Taking. Journal of Labor Economics, 20, pp. 877–898.

Hvide, H. K. and Kristiansen, E. G. (2003): Risk Taking in selection contests. Games and Economic Behavior, 42, pp. 172–179.

Johnson, E. J., Camerer, C., Sen, S. and Rymon, T. (2002): Detecting Failures of Backward Induction: Monitoring Information Search in Sequential Bargaining. Journal of Economic Theory, 104, pp. 16–47.

Kempf, A., Ruenzi, S. and Thiele, T. (forthcoming): Employment Risk, Compensation Incentives and Managerial Risk Taking - Evidence from the Mutual Fund Industry. Journal of Financial Economics.

Knoeber, C. R. and Thurman, W. N. (1994): Testing the Theory of Tournaments: An Empirical Analysis of Broiler Production. Journal of Labor Economics, 12, pp. 155–179.

Konrad, K. A. (2007): Strategy in Contests - An Introduction. WZB Discussion Paper SP II 2007-01.

Koski, J. L. and Pontiff, J. (1999): How are Derivatives used? Evidence from the Mutual Fund Industry. Journal of Finance, 54, pp. 791–816.

Kräkel, M. (forthcoming): Optimal risk taking in an uneven tournament game between risk averse players. Journal of Mathematical Economics.

Kräkel, M., Nieken, P. and Przemeck, J. (2008): Risk-Taking in Winner-Take-All Competition. Working Paper.

Kräkel, M. and Sliwka, D. (2004): Risk Taking in Asymmetric Tournaments. German Economic Review, 5, pp. 103–116.

Lazear, E. P. and Rosen, S. (1981): Rank-Order Tournaments as Optimum Labor Contracts. Journal of Political Economy, 89, pp. 841–864.

Lee, K., Lev, B. and Yeo, G. (2008): Executive pay dispersion, corporate governance, and firm performance. Review of Quantitative Finance and Accounting, 30, pp. 315–338.

Main, B. G., O'Reilly, C. A. and Wade, J. (1993): Top Executive Pay: Tournament or Teamwork. Journal of Labor Economics, 11, pp. 606–628.

Malcomson, J. M. (1984): Work Incentives, Hierarchy, and Internal Labor Markets. Journal of Political Economy, 92, pp. 486–507.

Malcomson, J. M. (1986): Rank-Order Contracts for a Principal with Many Agents. Review of Economic Studies, 53, pp. 807–817.

Moldovanu, B. and Sela, A. (2001): The Optimal Allocation of Prizes in Contests. American Economic Review, 91, pp. 542–558.

Moore, M. L. (1973): Management Changes and Discretionary Accounting Decisions. Journal of Accounting Research, 11, pp. 100–107.

Murphy, K. J. (1999): Executive Compensation. In: Ashenfelter, O. and Card, D. (Ed.) Handbook of Labor Economics, Volume 3, North-Holland, Amsterdam.

Murphy, W. H., Dacin, P. A. and Ford, N. M. (2004): Sales Contest Effectiveness: An Examination of Sales Contest Design Preferences of Field Sales Forces. Journal of the Academy of Marketing Science, 32, pp. 127–143.

Nagel, R. (1995): Unraveling in Guessing Games: An Experimental Study. American Economic Review, 85, pp. 1313–1326.

Nalebuff, B. J. and Stiglitz, J. E. (1983): Prizes and Incentives: Towards a General Theory of Compensation and Competition. Bell Journal of Economics, 1, pp. 21–43.

Nieken, P. (2008): On the Choice of Risk and Effort in Tournaments - Experimental Evidence. Working Paper.

Nieken, P. and Sliwka, D. (2007): Risk-Taking Tournaments - Theory and Experimental Evidence. Working Paper.

Nieken, P. and Sliwka, D. (2008): Management Changes and Big Bath Earnings Management. Working Paper.

O'Keeffe, M., Viscusi, W. and Zeckhauser, R. (1984): Economic Contests: Comparative Reward Schemes. Journal of Labor Economics, 2, pp. 27–56.

O'Reilly, C. A., Main, B. M. and Crystal, G. (1988): CEO Compensation as Tournament and Social Comparison: A Tale of Two Stories. Administrative Science Quarterly, 33, pp. 357–374.

Orszag, J. M. (1994): A New Look at Incentive Effects and Golf Tournaments. Economic Letters, 46, pp. 77–88.

Pourciau, S. (1993): Earnings Management and Nonroutine Executive Changes. Journal of Accounting and Economics, 16, pp. 317–336.

Qui, J. (2003): Termination Risk, Multiple Managers and Mutual Fund Tournaments. European Finance Review, 7, pp. 461–492.

Reitenga, A. L. and Tearney, M. G. (2003): Mandatory CEO Retirements, Discretionary Accruals, and Corporate Governance Mechanisms. Journal of Accounting, Auditing & Finance, 18, pp. 255–280.

Ronen, J. and Yaari, V. (2008): Earnings Management: Emerging Insights in Theory, Practice, and Research. Springer, New York.

Schipper, K. (1989): Commentary on Earnings Management. Accounting Horizons, 3, pp. 91–102.

Schotter, A. and Weigelt, K. (1992): Asymmetric tournaments, equal opportunity laws, and affirmative action: some experimental results. Quarterly Journal of Economics, 107, pp. 511–539.

Selten, R. (1978): The Chain Store Paradox. Theory and Decision, 9, pp. 127–159.

Selten, R. and Stoecker, R. (1986): End Behavior in Sequences of Finite Prisoner's Dilemma Supergames. Journal of Economic Behavior and Organization, 7, pp. 47–70.

Shuto, A. (2007): Executive compensation and earnings management: Empirical evidence from Japan. Journal of International Accounting, Auditing, and Taxation, 16, pp. 1–26.

Strong, J. S. and Meyer, J. R. (1987): Asset Writedowns: Managerial Incentives and Security Returns. Journal of Finance, 42, pp. 643–663.

Sunde, U. (2003): Potential, Prizes and Performance: Testing Tournament Theory with Professional Tennis Data. IZA Discussion Paper No. 947, Bonn.

Szymanski, S. (2003): The Economic Design of Sporting Contests. Journal of Economic Literature, 41, pp. 1137–1187.

Taylor, J. (2003): Risk-taking behavior in mutual fund tournaments. Journal of Economic Behavior and Organization, 50, pp. 373–383.

Waerneryd, K. (2000): In Defense of Lawyers: Moral Hazard as an Aid to Cooperation. Games and Economic Behavior, 33, pp. 145–158.

Walsh, P. (1991): "Big Bath Accounting" Using Extraordinary Items Adjustments: Empirical Australian Evidence. Journal of Business Finance & Accounting, 18, pp. 173–189.

Weisbach, M. S. (1995): CEO turnover and the firm's investment decisions. Journal of Financial Economics, 37, pp. 159–188.

Wells, P. (2002): Earnings management surrounding CEO changes. Accounting and Finance, 42, pp. 169–193.

Wu, S. and Roe, B. (2005): Behavioral and Welfare Effects of Tournaments and Fixed Performance Contracts: Some Experimental Evidence. American Journal of Agricultural Economies, 87, pp. 130–146.

Zhou, H. (2006): R & D Tournaments with Spillovers. Atlantic Economic Journal, 34, pp. 327–339.